THE THEOLOGY OF NAHMANIDES SYSTEMATICALLY PRESENTED

Number 271

THE THEOLOGY OF NAHMANIDES SYSTEMATICALLY PRESENTED

by
David Novak

THE THEOLOGY OF NAHMANIDES SYSTEMATICALLY PRESENTED

by

DAVID NOVAK
University of Virginia

Scholars Press
Atlanta, Georgia

THE THEOLOGY OF NAHMANIDES SYSTEMATICALLY PRESENTED

by
David Novak

Library of Congress Cataloging-in-Publication Data
Novak, David. 1941-
The theology of Nahmanides systematically presented/ by David Novak.
p. cm. — (Brown Judaic studies; no. 271) (Studies in medieval Judaism; v. 2)
Includes bibliographical references and indexes.
ISBN: 1-55540-802-8 (cloth)
1. Nahmanides, ca. 1195-ca. 1270. 2. Judaism—History of doctrines. I. Title. II. Series. III. Series: Studies in medieval Judaism; v. 2.
BM755.M62N68 1993
296.3—dc20 92-35709
CIP
978-1-930675-59-9 (pbk. : alk. paper)

Printed in the United States of America
on acid-free paper

STUDIES IN MEDIEVAL JUDAISM

Edited by

Lenn E. Goodman

To the Memory of

Harry H. Ruskin

(1905-1989)

The righteous man lives in his faith.

– Habakkuk 2:4

other works by David Novak

Law and Theology in Judaism (2 volumes)

Suicide and Morality

The Image of the Non-Jew in Judaism

Halakhah in a Theological Dimension

Jewish Christian Dialogue

Contents

Editor's Foreword

This volume is the second of the Studies in Medieval Judaism series within Brown Judaic Studies. The author, David Novak, one of the foremost living exponents of Jewish theology and social thought, here examines the ideas of Rabbi Moses ben Nahman (1194-1270), the Ramban, Nahmanides in the European literature. An exegete, epistemologist of Jewish history and experience, and pioneer of Kabbalistic reasoning, Nahmanides was the spokesperson of embattled Spanish Jewry at the ominous Barcelona disputation before King James of Aragon in 1263. He was the first major rabbi to treat resettlement of the Land of Israel as a Biblical commandment. Inspired by the ideal of the poet philosopher Judah Halevi, whose theories of Jewish history and destiny so influenced his own, Nahmanides left an increasingly anti-Jewish Spain and spent his final years in the Land of Israel.

Like many of his contemporaries, Nahmanides found himself in opposition to the bold rationalism of Maimonides (1135-1204). He was a Talmudist who found limitless scope in exploration of the canon that Maimonides saw not as an end in itself but as a guide to the material, moral and spiritual fulfillment of his people. The present book calls out frequent examples of Nahmanides' explicit and implicit criticism of Maimonidean positions. But in the controversy that surrounded Maimonides' halakhic and philosophic writings after his death, Nahmanides sought a moderating and conciliating role, urging dispassionate judgment, defending anti-Maimonists from the zeal of their detractors, but supporting Maimonides' thesis that God transcends physicality against those who couched the extremity of their reaction to philosophy in affirmations of divine corporeality.

Nahmanides saw more clearly than many that even for those who might reach conclusions at variance with the themes to which Maimonides' thought had led him, it was Maimonides who laid out the problematics of Jewish philosophy most decisively and who framed the issues as all subsequent thinkers would have to confront them. Although his sympathies leaned strongly in the direction of history, revelation, and experience, as counterweights to the rationalistic faith of the Rambam, Nahmanides was never an adversary of reason. His aim was to soften and supplement its claims from the rich store of prophetic experience and rabbinic thought. His exegetical impulses were pluralistic and open-minded; and his creative work in kabbalistic exegesis–above all, in promulgating and developing the ancient theme that the life of the commandments allows us to participate in the life of God, and indeed contributes to that life–springs from a wholesome and rationalistic desire to situate the commandments within a comprehensive cosmology, ontology and axiology. So there is no paradox in Joseph Sarachek's observation that, "It was a cabalist, Nahmanides, who saved Maimonides in the hectic days of 1232." Indeed, the Kabbalah itself is a vehicle of Maimonidean and more broadly neoplatonic philosophical themes.

What David Novak has done here is to survey the canon of Nahmanides' writings–commentaries, discourses, sermons, even the record made by the Ramban of his Barcelona disputation–to elicit the structure of a systematic theology. Nahmanides, admittedly, was no system builder. As Novak shows, he often subordinated perfect consistency to the nuances he discovered in a text. He willingly sacrificed the chance to enlarge some favorite speculative theme to the material message he found in tradition. In this he reveals that penchant for the empirical that he shares not only with Halevi but with Saadiah. Like both of them, he relies on an idea of experience that is not merely personal but communal and thus can span the generations and even rein in the exuberance of reason.

Yet we see most clearly that Nahmanides is no obscurantist and indeed no anti-rationalist, when we observe him working with a text and finding in it multiple levels of meaning, preferring the subtler, not ignoring the more obvious and accessible, and never giving preference to the merely homiletic or the purely positive over the reading that might shed light on God's inner purposes. While he is not a system builder with a capital S, Nahmanides is a coherent thinker with a distinctive repertoire of themes and commitments that emerge powerfully from David Novak's thematically sensitive selection and careful translation, arrangement and discussion of the key passages of his work. Placement of Nahmanides' thoughts on a systematic footing reveals him as a major theologian, both creative and loyal to the tradition that inspirits him. This book thus fulfills its author's aim when it guides not only historical scholars but contemporary thinkers along the pathways of a rich vein of Jewish theological insight, whose internal structure and integrity are all too readily overlooked by readers who encounter Nahmanides only in the exegesis of particular verses or in the dialectics of some historic debate. It shows us a Nahmanides still capable, after seven hundred years, of contributing vitally to Jewish theology as a living enterprise and a continuing adventure.

Lenn E. Goodman
Manoa Valley, September 1992

Preface

In introducing a recent collection of papers on Nahmanides' thought, Isadore Twersky writes, "great is the literary oeuvre of Ramban, embracing as it does halakah, aggadah, Scriptural exegesis, homilies, kabbalah, philosophy, poetry, polemics.... we should mention also his intensive activity as communal leader and spokesman for Spanish Jewry during prolonged periods of internal crisis, antagonism and strife as well as external oppression and turbulence."[1] Given the immensity of Nahmanides' achievement, a definitive study of his work covering all these areas in detail and leading to a general synthesis has yet to be written. This book does not pretend to such comprehensiveness. My task here is the more modest one of uncovering the theology that guides Nahmanides in his exegetical work and informs his reading of Scriptural and rabbinic texts. I hope that this book will prove helpful to students interested in discerning an overall picture of Nahmanides' theology and to the readers of his works.

The main elements of Nahmanides' theology are set forth in the divisions of this book. Each section is based on selections from the texts where the relevant ideas are most clearly presented. In searching for the central themes, I have examined all of Nahmanides' extant writings, but most of the passages chosen are from his *magnum opus*, the *Commentary on the Torah*, which was the culmination of his life's work.[2] Accompanying these selections are introductory notes and sometimes an endnote. The former sketch the conceptual point made by the Ramban and suggest its role in the context of his thought. The latter seek to situate the point he is making, either by comparison or by contrast, in the larger context of Jewish tradition.

I have tried to see the issues as perennial ones, so that contemporary readers who are interested in Jewish theology – even committed to it – can better see Nahmanides' views as options within an ongoing enterprise. That, indeed, is the main purpose of this book. It is inspired by (but hardly comparable to) the efforts of the classical codifiers of Jewish law, who reorganized great volumes of heterogenous Talmudic material along more recognizably conceptual lines.[3] Their purpose was to make the material more readily available for the normative tasks of their day and the future. In attempting to adopt the methodological model of the classical codifiers, I am expressing a commitment to the view that theology is a normative task for Jewish thinkers today.

To lay out the elements of Nahmanides' theology systematically requires transposing passages from their original contexts. Nahmanides himself did not write a comprehensive treatise on theology. The closest he came was a short work called *Torat ha-Shem Temimah,* which was in fact a long sermon he preached in Barcelona in 1263 just before his famous disputation with the apostate Jew Pablo Christiani before King James of Aragon and his court. But this work, much influenced by Judah Halevi, presents only Nahmanides' theology of history. It deals especially with public miracles and the meaning of those commandments that seem intended to commemorate and celebrate them. It does not deal with the other two main strands of Nahmanides' religious thought: his rationalist themes, which have strong affinities with the ideas of Saadiah Gaon, and the crucial and distinctive kabbalistic elements in his theology. Moreover, the sermon does not reveal how deeply his ongoing critique of Maimonides stimulated his original theological insights. Thus a translation of *Torat ha-Shem Temimah,* or even a discussion of its major points, would not adequately represent the richness of Nahmanides' theology.

In reconstructing that theology on systematic lines, I have resorted as much as possible to the relevant secondary scholarship – most of it of rather recent issue. Even so, the selection and ordering of texts cannot help but appear somewhat arbitrary. Yet because I am convinced that our own discussions in Jewish theology can be greatly enriched by the insights of Nahmanides, I persevered in the arduous and often uncertain task of selecting and ordering his diverse comments and remarks and coping with his notoriously difficult Hebrew style. The fundamentally exegetical nature of Nahmanides' project and his difficult style of writing render his insights less accessible today than those of more systematic Jewish theologians like Saadiah Gaon, Judah Halevi, Maimonides, the author of the *Zohar,* Gersonides, Hasdai ibn Crescas, Joseph Albo, Isaac Abrabanel, Moses Cordovero, Elijah Benamozegh, Hermann Cohen, or Franz Rosenzweig. My task, as I see it, is to help remedy Nahmanides' present undeserved obscurity.

My interest in Nahmanides began at the age of sixteen, when as a Talmud student in Chicago I was first introduced to his *Commentary on the Torah* by my pious teacher, Rabbi Curt Peritz, whose reverence for Nahmanides was clearly marked by his always calling him *Der Ramban Kaudesch.* I echo his distinctive German pronunciation of the name as I so often heard it, "the holy Rabbi Moses ben Nahman." His reverence for Nahmanides stemmed from the influence of Rabbi Moses Schreiber (the

Hatam Sofer, d. 1839), in whose yeshivah in Bratislava, Czechoslovakia (formerly, Pressburg, Hungary) my teacher had studied under the spiritual and lineal descendents of the Hatam Sofer in the years just following the First World War. For it was the Hatam Sofer who greatly urged that the works of Nahmanides be rescued from obscurity and restored to centralility in the curriculum of rabbinic scholars.[4]

As a student in the Jewish Theological Seminary of America during the years 1961-1966, I was privileged to take part in a special research program in Jewish theology led by my late revered teacher, Abraham Joshua Heschel. During my last year there I was assigned the task of intense study of the works of Nahmanides, especially his disputes with Maimonides.[5] That experience focused my lifelong interest in this body of thought. Over the years I have returned to Nahmanides again and again, both in my research on questions of Jewish law and theology, and also for insights into the weekly readings of the Torah, upon which it was my privilege to preach during the more than twenty years I served as a pulpit rabbi.

So it was a welcome invitation when my close friend and colleague, Lenn E. Goodman of the University of Hawaii, the editor of Studies in Medieval Judaism for the Brown Judaic Studies Series, asked me to write this little book on Nahmanides' theology. I am deeply grateful to Professor Goodman for his patience in waiting for the manuscript (which was far too long in coming), his extraordinary care in editing it (both as regards substance and style), and his continual encouragement of this work and others. Our friendship over the years, sustained over an enormous geographic distance, has demonstrated to me the truth of Aristotle's insight that intellectual friendship is friendship at its very best.

I owe much to David Berger of Brooklyn College, a distinguished scholar of Nahmanides' thought, who read the entire manuscript and taught me much by his insightful and learned comments. I am appreciative too for the helpful comments of two anonymous readers of the manuscript I prepared. Since Nahmanides was one of the great Talmudists of all times, my understanding of his use of rabbinic texts has profited from my many discussions with one of the great Talmudists of our own time, my friend, David Weiss Halivni of Columbia University, now also the Rector of the Institute of Traditional Judaism, where he and I are both privileged to teach. I feel obligated to express thanks here also to a deceased scholar whom I never knew personally, Charles B. Chavel. We both served as rabbis in Far Rockaway, New York, but at different times. All students of the works of Nahmanides today owe a debt of gratitude to the painstaking efforts of the late Rabbi Chavel in providing us with carefully edited versions of most of Nahmanides' works, along with many useful cross references to the vast Nahmanidean corpus and the works of his predecessors, contemporaries and successors.

This book is dedicated to the memory of my teacher, mentor and friend, Harry H. Ruskin. Like Nahmanides, he was not afraid to plumb the depths of the Torah. The purity of his faith, the power of his mind, and the nobility of his character inspired me when he was alive and continue to inspire me after his death. May his memory be blessed!

University of Virginia
Charlottesville

Sivan 5752/June 1992.

Introduction

1. *Rabbi Moses ben Nahman Gerondi*

Rabbi Moses ben Nahman Gerondi is known in Hebrew literature by his acronym Ramban. But to modern readers of European languages he is Nahmanides, and to his Spanish contemporaries he was Bonastruc da Porta. Each of his names tells something about his career. As Rabbi Moses ben Nahman Gerondi he was the most influential rabbinical leader of the Jews of Spain in his time. As the Ramban he has been a mainstay of Jewish thought throughout the centuries since his death. As Nahmanides he is gaining increasing recognition among students of Western religious thought. And as Bonastruc da Porta he played a central role in the complex relations between Spanish Jewry and the Christian society in which they lived.

Nahmanides was born in 1194 in Gerona, a small but culturally vital Jewish community near Barcelona, the capital of Aragon. He was descended from an aristocratic rabbinical family and was educated in Talmud and Kabbalah by leading scholars. Achieving a reputation as a brilliant rabbinic scholar at a very young age, he was widely consulted on halakhic and theological questions, and his introduction of the works of the tosafists of Northern France into the curriculum of his academy revolutionized Talmudic scholarship by synthesizing Sephardic and Ashkenazic traditions. His endorsement of Kabbalah, which was just beginning to emerge in Spain in his day, enhanced its respectability and broadened its audience. In the controversy over Maimonides' theological works in the first third of the thirteenth century, his efforts toward a compromise helped to preserve the access of traditional Jews to these works and fostered the integration we now take for granted of the thought of Maimonides into the generally conservative canon of Rabbinic literature.

After beginning his career in Gerona, Nahmanides served as the chief rabbinical authority of Catalonia. Although earning his living as a physician, he was a highly effective rabbi, teaching advanced students, deciding questions of Halakhah and social policy, preaching, and publishing a large body of work. As the leading Jewish scholar in Northern Spain, he was summoned in 1263 by King James of Aragon to dispute publicly with Pablo Christiani, a Jewish apostate who had become a Dominican friar. The topic was a dangerous one: the messiahship of Jesus. The disputation, held in the presence of the king and his court before an audience filled with dignitaries, took place in July in Barcelona. Its outcome was awaited anxiously by both Jews and Christians.

Astoundingly, the King deemed Nahmanides' defense of the Jewish refusal to accept Jesus as the Messiah as more convincing than Christiani's arguments. But the victory was pyrrhic. Strong pressures from the Dominicans forced Nahmanides to leave Aragon, and finally in 1267 he emigrated to the Land of Israel. He landed in Acre and soon settled in Jerusalem. As in Spain, he soon attracted many students, and his influence once again became widespread. He devoted the last years of his life to rebuilding the tiny and demoralized Jewish community of the Land into a center of higher Jewish learning.

Before his death in 1270, he completed his great life's work, the *Commentary on the Torah*, tying together the many strands of thought begun in his earlier works. Although this *magnum opus* contains a wealth of literary, exegetical, halakhic, historical and philological material, its theology gives it its profundity and its most abiding interest for Jewish thought and for the larger world.

2. *The Reasons for the Commandments*

We discover the heart of Nahmanides' theology in his theory of the commandments.[6] The need for the text of the Torah to be as normative as possible is the main incentive for *derash*, the method developed by the rabbis for unlocking the deeper and wider meaning of the text of Scripture. This method has been used for discovery both of the more precise norms governing action (*Halakhah*) and of the less precise norms guiding thought (*Aggadah*).[7] Inevitably, the search for deeper and wider norms involves the search for the underlying purposes of the Torah, *ta'amei ha-mitsvot*, the "reasons for the commandments." For if the commandments are to be expanded, an orderly elaboration requires some sense of the purposes the divine Lawgiver intended by them.[8] Indeed, the search for the reasons of the commandments is an objective counterpart of the subjective requirement that one who performs a commandment do so with proper intention (*kavvanah*).

Kavvanah operates on two levels. The first is the intention of fulfilling a divine commandment; this is called *kavvanah le-mitsvah*).[9] It is because the intention at this level is general that the same formula is used in the benediction required at the performance of most positive commandments:

"who sanctified us with his commandments and commanded us to –." What is intended is obedience to the will of God, irrespective of the specific commandment. A deeper level of *kavvanah* makes reference to the specific purpose of *this* commandment and focuses on how one comes closer to God by performing this specific act. This is called "the intention of the heart," *kavvanat ha-lev*.[10] It requires our apprehension, however limited, of the wisdom of God. It is in pursuing this deeper *kavvanah* that the search for the reasons of the commandments finds a more spiritual motivation than sheer intellectual curiosity.

It is the proper intention of the heart that distinguishes authentic religious actions from what my late revered teacher, Abraham Joshua Heschel, following up on a central theme of Bahya Ibn Paquda's, called "religious behaviorism".[11] Thus, when questioning why the Torah needs a general commandment "you shall be holy" (Lev. 19:2), inasmuch as all the commandments are designed to make us holy, Nahmanides makes the striking observation that one can "be a wretch within the parameters of what the Torah permits" (*naval bi-rshut ha-Torah*).[12] The mere observance of the legalities does not insure one of becoming a holy person, which is the ultimate purpose of the commandments.

Nahmanides is not arguing, of course, that holiness can be attained without observing the Torah.[13] The specific obligations of the Law are indispensable for the human fulfillment that it intends.[14] Yet the requirement of *kavvanah* indicates that the Torah is concerned with much more than behavioral observance. In fact, in this particular passage, Nahmanides shows how the intention of holiness should lead one to do more than the letter of the law requires.

The rationalist Jewish theology of the Middle Ages, especially when influenced by Aristotelian teleology, provided a stimulus and a method to the search for the reasons of the commandments. It assumed that there are always purposes both in nature and in human activities. Thus Maimonides saw all of the commandments as seeking the improvement of the body and society (*tiqqun ha-guf*) or the improvement of the soul (*tiqqun ha-nefesh*).[15] In the third section of his *Guide of the Perplexed*, he argued that the reasons for all the specific commandments could be located under these general rubrics.

Impressive as this method of inquiry can be intellectually, it bears with it some religious dangers. For example, in the *Guide* Maimonides emphasizes the filthy conditions in which pigs live, making pork a food unwholesome for the body.[16] But the same reason might be used to avoid the prohibition, if one could show that it is possible to raise pigs hygienically. If the prohibition serves some mere natural need, that need might be met without, say, avoiding pork. Similarly, when the reason for a commandment is taken to be the improvement of the soul. If, for example, the purpose of the commandment to study the Torah is to apprehend metaphysical truths which can be apprehended, in principle, by anyone of moral probity and intellectual ability, what prevents general metaphysics from displacing the study of the Torah as the highest human activity?[17]

Maimonides clearly emphasized the authority of the commandments regardless of one's apprehension of their reasons.[18] Still, there were religious concerns about the practical neglect of the commandments to which his philosophical approach could (and probably did) lend itself. Such concerns led the rabbis of Northern France actually to ban the study of Maimonides' theological writings. The "Maimonidean Controversy" that ensued, came to a head in 1232, the rabbinic world seemingly polarized between pro and anti-Maimonists.[19] The thirty-eight year old Nahmanides, already a halakhic authority respected in all quarters of the Jewish world, attempted a compromise.

Although himself concerned about the dangers of a philosophical approach to the commandments, Nahmanides defended Maimonides, arguing that his rationalist theology was not intended for the masses of faithful Jews, but only for those who had been exposed to philosophy and so required philosophical justifications as a condition of their own religious stability.[20] Nahmanides clearly agreed with Maimonides that there are reasons for all the commandments. He differed with him, and with all other rationalist Jewish theologians, in his insistence that the reasons for the commandments are not grounded in metaphysics but in uniquely Jewish facts.[21] The project of eliciting these foundations is carried forward in all his writings and becomes the major theme of his crowning achievement, the *Commentary on the Torah*, which he began in Spain before his exile and completed not long before his death in the Land of Israel in 1270.

3. *Commandments Based on Nature and Reason*

Some scholars have assumed that Nahmanides' opposition to Greek metaphysics, especially that of Aristotle, means that he could not accept the reality of any natural order. Since the ideas of natural order and universally valid human reason are correlative, it would seem that rejection of nature immediately leads to rejection of reason. So it is concluded that Nahmanides was an "anti-rationalist."[22] But Nahmanides did not reject a natural order or universal human reason.[23] What he did reject was the assumption of some theologians that nature/reason must be constituted according to the categories of Aristotle. His main objection to Aristotle and his Jewish followers was that they assumed that the natural order is all-encompassing and that universal reason suffices for our knowledge of all things, including God. Aristotle and the Jewish Aristotelians seemed to leave no room for creation or revelation, at least as Nahmanides understood these doctrines.

For Nahmanides, rejection of Aristotelian metaphysics did not lead to the rejection of nature or to anti-rationalism but to a more circumscribed conception of the range of nature and scope of reason. In some ways

Nahmanides was more rationalist than Maimonides. Operating within a more limited range, he could more easily demonstrate the truth of reason's claims. This difference is notable in regard to commandments governing interhuman relationships (*bayn adam le-ḥavero*).

The advantages of Nahmanides' approach are manifest, for example, if we compare his treatment of the Seven Noahide Commandments with that of Maimonides. The Noahide Commandments are those laws which the rabbis considered binding on all humankind, the "sons of Noah."[24] These laws, prohibiting murder, incest and robbery, among other crimes, are acknowledged in virtually all societies and are readily seen as requirements of reason. Many Jewish theologians call them rational commandments (*mitsvot sikhliyot*).[25] They belong to what later Jewish thinkers (following Stoic and Christian philosophers) identified as natural law.[26]

In a famous passage in the *Mishneh Torah*, Maimonides states that anyone who accepts these laws only by dint of ordinary reason (*hekhrea ha-da'at*) is not deemed worthy of the bliss of the world-to-come, in which "the pious of the nations of the world" are assured a share.[27] In his earlier *Commentary on the Mishnah*, Maimonides seems to reject the very concept of "rational commandments."[28] Some scholars see in these two passages a rejection of any natural law morality. But a better argument can be made that Maimonides was in fact rejecting only a natural law morality not grounded in adequate understanding of the true metaphysical constitution of nature.[29] He was rejecting the religious soundness (although not, perhaps, the political usefulness) of norms discovered or invented by prudence rather than by insight about God and the universe.

According to this approach, the only truly adequate morality is one whose metaphysical grounds are sound and properly understood, and the only truly effective metaphysics is one whose moral consequences are sound and properly understood. For Maimonides there is a strong rational connection between metaphysics and morals.[30] Metaphysics is the deepest ground of morality. It is what makes morality natural rather than merely human legislation. And morality is the most useful fruit of metaphysics. Without morality, metaphysics has no practical or political influence. Without metaphysics, morality has no universal foundation. Thus, in Maimonides' view, metaphysics is more than just theoretical; and morality is more than just practical. The two are linked by reason, and so discoverable from one another by proper use of reason.

Nahmanides did not see any such rational connection between metaphysics and morality. Indeed, his theology leaves hardly any place for metaphysics. The deepest truths about the universe are reached only via revelation. The moral norms evident to reason are those required by any society to fulfill the basic needs of its members for a just and stable order. Ultimately, of course, such a morality must be included in the revealed law. But revelation comes at unique historical junctures, not through constant natural processes, so it cannot function as a rational ground for morality.

Revelation is not, like reason, the discovery of the constant order of the universe. So reason, for Nahmanides, cannot bridge the gap between revelation and morality, as it can bridge the gap between metaphysics and morality for Maimonides.

Yet, as a result of this sundering of metaphysics from morality, the rationality of natural morality is heightened, not lessened in Nahmanides' theology. Maimonides seems to require profound metaphysical insight before the most elemental moral truths acquire their full significance. For Nahmanides, whatever morality humans can learn for themselves is much more directly known. Thus Nahmanides comments, fairly typically:

> Violence is robbery and oppression... for violence is a sin, as is known and universally accepted (*ve-ha-mefursam*).... the reason is that its prohibition is a rational obligation (*mitsvah muskelet*), for which there is no need for a prophet to give a commandment.[31]

Nahmanides accepts the legitimacy of natural law on the interhuman level. But such morality and revelation are not located on the same plane. Morality comes *from* humans (at least in its most elemental manifestations). Revelation comes *to* them. Before Sinai, Nahmanides argues,

> You find that the patriarchs and prophets conducted themselves in an evidently moral manner (*derekh 'erets*).... and inference *a fortiori*, if the patriarchs and the prophets who came to do God's will conducted themselves in an evidently moral manner, how much more so should ordinary people![32]

Morality does not itself lead to revelation, although it is a precondition for it. Morality will not anticipate in any detail either the event of revelation or its rich content.

4. *Commandments Based on History*

Those commandments whose reasons seem evident are called *mishpatim*, "judgments." Their locus is the relationship among human beings in daily life. But for Nahmanides the realm of nature (including our political nature) is not where the true relationship between God and human beings is to be found. Nature, as philosophically or scientifically conceived, is a constant order; it does not admit of innovation. But the most elemental fact about God to be recognized by his creatures is that God is the Creator; the universe is the result of his absolutely free act. God can intervene in his universe at any time, regardless of the familiar order of nature. That order is only *usual*. It has no inherent or intrinsic necessity.

This anti-metaphysical point, made by Nahmanides in the thirteenth century was made by David Hume with a different intent in the eighteenth.[33] It is to teach us that the natural order has no ultimate necessity that the Torah places such stress on miracles. For it is through miracles, especially those of a spectacular kind (*nissim mefursamim*), that God demonstrates his power over the universe he created.[34]

Yet these spectacular miracles occurred centuries ago, and even then they were performed rarely. What connection does the ordinary Jew have with such great events? How do they become a personal experience and so impart an appreciation of God's creative power and providence? Nahmanides sees the Torah's solution to this problem in those commandments called *'edot*, "testimonies," commandments based on history. Glossing the commandment that the Exodus "be a sign upon your hand and a symbol between your eyes, for with a strong hand the Lord brought us out of Egypt" (Exod. 13:16), which rabbinic tradition saw as mandating the regular wearing of *tefillin*, Nahmanides writes:

> This is because God does not perform a sign (*'ot*) and demonstration (*mofet*) in every generation, to be seen by every evildoer and denier (*kofer*). Rather, he commands us continually to perform a memorial (*zikaron*) and sign of what our eyes saw.[35]

Nahmanides here voices a participatory view of history. This perspective, which he often restates, contrasts sharply with the more familiar, illustrative view of history. Our social sciences, modelling themselves on the natural sciences, typically seek regularities in human behavior and attempt to see all events as examplars of constant processes. History thus becomes a gathering of data from the past to broaden the number of examples that illustrate various specific principles. Interest in the past is governed by the interests of the present and their projection into the future.[36]

Nahmanides' view of history reflects a much more ancient assumption. Human life in the present, including all the normal processes of human behavior, derives its meaning from great events in the past. The task of history is not to incorporate the events of the past into perennial patterns discernable in the present and projected into the future but to see the processes of the present as marks and symbols of the great events of the past.[37] For Jews, this incorporation of the present into the past is the function of those commandments that symbolically reenact the great (and rare) past events.

Emphasizing our symbolic participation in the great events when God made himself so powerfully manifest to the people of Israel, Nahmanides indicates that this participation is not just passively experienced. It requires the determination to act with an openness to the divine presence when and where it has revealed itself. God does not perform his mighty acts routinely, lest we become passive spectators rather than active participants. For those who deny God's providential power, even regular performance of miracles and signs would be wasted. Obstinacy would block their message.[38] But, for those who have an underlying propensity for faith, the activation of that propensity demands symbolic participation.

It is with such themes in mind that Nahmanides writes about Abraham's "trial," stressing the importance of action rather than mere passive good will:

> A trial (*nisayon*) is called by this name because of the one who is tried. But the one who tries him, may He be exalted, commands it in order to bring matter from potentiality to actuality, so that the one tried may receive the reward action deserves, not just the reward for having a good heart... and so indeed it is with all the trials in the Torah. They are for the good of the one who is tried."[39]

Like the commandments based on nature (*mishpatim*), the historically based commandments (*'edot*) fulfill human needs. The *mishpatim* fulfill the needs of humans in their relations with one another in society; the *'edot* fulfill the needs of humans in their relationship with God in history.[40] Ordinary people need to share in the experience of the spectacular public miracles of history, either directly or symbolically, in order to appreciate God's transcendence of the natural order and their own capacity for transcending it, even if only partially.

Among Nahmanides' predecessors, his rather empirical view of nature comes closest to the view of Saadiah Gaon (d. 942). His view of history and its significance comes closest to that of Judah Halevi (d. 1140), whose influence he acknowledged.[41]

5. *The Metasocial/Metahistorical Commandments and Kabbalah*

The commandments of the Torah designated as *huqqim*, "statutes," have always posed a special challenge to those who are committed to the view that all the commandments of the Torah have reasons. For these commandments seem to be arbitrary expressions of God's will. As one seminal midrash put it, God in effect says to the people of Israel, "I have enacted a statute (*huqqah haqqaqti*), I have decreed a decree (*gezerah gazarti*), and you are not permitted to transgress my decrees!"[42] This is stated in the context of a discussion of the institution in the Torah generally acknowledged as the most enigmatic, the rite of the Red Heifer (Numbers 19:1-22). Yet the midrash here seems to regard the ritual as paradigmatic of all the Torah's commandments.

Another midrash seems similarly to generalize from the pattern of the *huqqim* and announce that all the commandments were given only to test human acceptance of God's will:[43] The rabbis picture Satan and the nations of the world taunting the Jewish people for their tenacious fidelity to these mysterious commandments.[44] Such passages clearly place the burden of proof on those who affirm that all the commandments of the Torah do have reasons, however obscure. Rationalists are challenged to suggest at least some plausible reasons for the more problematic *huqqim* or else acknowledge that all the commandments are in essence divine decrees, and that even when there do seem to be reasons, these are at best surmisals or rationales, rather than primary groundings of God's true intent.[45]

But Maimonides and Nahmanides, both committed to the thesis that there are reasons for all the commandments, developed their own distinctive means of explaining the more difficult commandments of the Torah. It is at this level of exegetical challenge that their fundamental theological differences become most apparent. Indeed, it is against the background of Maimonides' treatment of these commandments that Nahmanides' position emerges most clearly by the contrast.

For Maimonides, truth and goodness are discovered through political science, physical science, or metaphysics.[46] His theology gives primacy to those commandments whose purposes are most evident to human reason: those that order society toward the good (*mishpatim*) or the mind toward the true (*de'ot*). The historical commandments (*'edot*) are set within this basic context. Thus observance of the Sabbath and festivals serves the political purpose of promoting fellowship through common leisure and celebration, and the intellectual purpose of signalling truths about the creation of the cosmos.[47] History, as a locus of God's revelation through unique events, is not an immediate consideration.[48]

Thus, for example, the Sabbath is instituted for the sake of remembering that "you were a slave in the land of Egypt, and the Lord your God brought you forth from there" (Deut. 5:15). But Maimonides stresses the Sabbath's universal significance: practically in fulfilling the physical need for rest; intellectually, in fulfilling the spiritual need to affirm God's creation of the universe.[49] Maimonides does invoke history when explaining some of the *huqqim*. He sees them as reactions to idolatry in ancient times.[50] Thus he gives two reasons for the prohibition of eating meat cooked in milk. First, he reasons that the high fat content of such food is unhealthful. Second, he surmises that cooking a kid in its dam's milk might well have been a pagan rite which the Torah did not want Israelites to imitate in any way.[51] As for the question why a reaction to a vanished pagan rite should remain normative, it should be remembered that Maimonides saw the propensity to idolatry as perennial. So even prohibitions of particular temporal manifestations of idolatry still serve to emphasize the importance of perpetual diligence against this ever virulent spiritual disease.[52]

For Maimonides, then, the rationally evident commandments are primary; the explicitly historical commandments are, in effect, dehistoricized; and the mysterious *huqqim* are seen as reactions to historical circumstances.

In his ordering of the commandments, it would seem that the *mishpatim* (political and intellectual) come first, the *'edot* second, and the *huqqim* third in importance. For Nahmanides, the order seems to be diametrically reversed. The *mishpatim* are least important, precisely because they are most universal. The *'edot* are more important, because they are more distinctive. And the *huqqim* are most important, since they are the most distinctive of all and sanctified by their very mystery.

Thus in explaining the *huqqim* Nahmanides invokes what he deems the true, deepest teaching of the Torah — Kabbalah. His reliance on Kabbalah has long been a subject of debate. Some scholars of a highly traditional cast believe that the *Zohar* is literally the work of the second-century Tanna Simeon bar Yohai. They hold that it was known immemorially and passed down hermetically by a small elite for a thousand years before its publication in the late thirteenth century. Such scholars think that Nahmanides' invocation of Kabbalah is highly selective. They hold that there is much more to his kabbalistic theology than he revealed in his writings.[53] Kabbalists often claim that the esoteric nature of Kabbalah requires such restraint. But even this view does not explain why Nahmanides invokes kabbalistic doctrines when and where he does–why what was revealed to kabbalists is most frequently used to explain the reasons for the *huqqim*.

Most modern scholars accept the view of Gershom Scholem that the *Zohar* is largely the work of Rabbi Moses de Leon, who wrote after Nahmanides and was influenced by him.[54] They ascribe Nahmanides' sporadic invocations of Kabbalah to the still unsystematic nature of the tradition and regard de Leon and his successors as the true systematizers.[55] There is no evidence that Nahmanides' kabbalism was systematic.[56] Unlike the later kabbalists, from de Leon on, Nahmanides never attempted to explain everything in the Torah in the light of Kabbalah. Unlike most of them, he regularly assumed the reality of nature and history in explaining the commandments and events in the Torah. Indeed, as we have seen, his use of nature in explaining the *mishpatim* approximates Saadiah Gaon's theory of rational commandments, and in his use of history in explaining the *'edot* follows Judah Halevi's conception of unique events.

The *Zohar*, by contrast, does not effectually admit a realm of nature or a realm of history. It takes all relations to be internal to the life of God.[57] Space and time are unreal. There is no history, no nature, in the sense of a lasting created order resulting from a unique divine act.[58] God's creation is no longer transitive, its object is not clearly distinct from its subject. For the post-Nahmanidean kabbalists, the only reality separate from God is demonic (literally, *sitra ahra*, "the other side"). Relationship with this is tantamount to annihilation.[59] Thus the *Zohar* treats the Seven Noahide commandments not as rational requirements of interhuman relations but as ultimate proscriptions of separation from the divine life.[60] Their specific interhuman dimensions become incidental.

Zoharic kabbalism leaves no room for the Saadian rationalism that Nahmanides used in constituting the natural law of interhuman relations. For such rationalism assumes created space outside God, the result of God's creation as a transitive act.[61] History again, presupposes an essential distinction between space and time.[62] In the idea of nature, space and time are linked. But the idea of freedom demands their separation, lest everything be determined. When time is seen as distinct from space, it is opens up the future as a horizon of actions not determined by what already is. This opening is crucial for the emergence of personal responsibility. In Nahmanides' view of history, as in Halevi's, history is an encounter between God and his creatures.[63] The relationship is free on God's part because it is not determined by the natural order. God's miracles recapitulate the original free act of creation and reaffirm God's transcendence. And the relationship is free on the part of human beings, because our response to God's presence is not determined by nature.[64] Responding to God's holy actions, we can choose to perform holy deeds. Holiness transcends what has already been made. Thus history is a story of events rather than the record of inevitable processes. Its trajectory is towards culmination in a transcendent world-to-come. This realm is not an eternal reality already present parallel to nature for Nahmanides, as it is for Maimonides. Rather it lies in the future. It will be completely new.[65]

Historically constituted freedom, then, is a transitive, undetermined power shared by God and humanity, although the freedom of the Creator is not constrained like that of creatures. Our observance of the commandments is almost always bounded within natural limits, unlike God's performance of miracles.[66] So divine and human freedom interact in the covenantal relationship, but not symmetrically. God always retains his limitlessness. Man is always limited. Without some structure, however, divine freedom would be mere caprice; all the more so, human freedom. Caprice is freedom that intends no relationship.

The alternatives to that terrifying possibility are to constitute a realm of covenantal history between God and man, or to constitute a nature within God, into which humans can be embedded. The later kabbalists chose the second option. But as a result, spontaneity and freedom were quickly lost. The determinism of nature was now projected into the Godhead itself. Miracles became events determined by this higher, implicit nature.[67] Human good became more and more a product of divine causal power[68]; human evil, more and more an outcome of the generalized power of the demonic rather than of specific human choices.[69]

Nahmanides is not content with such an outcome. His eclectic method enables him to shift his theological ground repeatedly. At times he locates the divine-human relation between God and man. At other times, especially when explaining the *huqqim*, he locates the relation within the Godhead. This shifting prevents us from reconstructing a consistent, systematic theology for Nahmanides, as one can for Saadiah, Maimonides, or the

Zohar. Yet Nahmanides' use of Kabbalah is consistent with the profound conservatism of his halakhic and theological writings.[70] For the higher truths of the Kabbalah, invoked as explications of the *huqqim*, pose little threat to nature or history and do not pretend to displace the broad truth of the Torah. Kabbalah in Nahmanides will not revolutionize Jewish theology through and through. But it will allow him profoundly to explain what earlier theologies had not explained or had explained inadequately. In the process, the *huqqim* are transformed from stumbling blocks of faith to symbolic hints of God's deep mysteries.

Opening his comments on Leviticus, where the Torah deals most fully with the sacrificial system, the context for so many of the *huqqim*, Nahmanides rejects Maimonides' historicization of the Biblical cult of sacrifice. He is convinced that Maimonides has read into the Scriptural texts a thematic that is not truly there. Maimonides had said that the reason for the sacrifices is that the Egyptians and Chaldeans, in whose land Israel had dwelt, "had always worshipped cattle and sheep [and goats]... because of this He commanded them to slaughter these three species for the sake of God, in order that it be known that what they had thought was the epitome of sin is that which they should now offer to the Creator.... And so will the corrupt beliefs, which are diseases of the soul, be cured, for every disease and every sickness is only cured by its opposite. – These are his words in which he spoke at length, but they are hollow words (*divrei hav'ai*)."[71]

Nahmanides offers two alternative explanations of the significance the Torah ascribes to the sacrificial system. The first is psychological and spiritual: The sacrifices satisfy the profound human need to be reconciled with God in thought, in word, and in deed. This interpretation is immediately attractive to the imagination; it "draws the heart."[72] Yet Nahmanides follows it by alluding to the *true*, kabbalistic view, which grows from the realization that the unique name of God (YHWH) and not his lesser names is invariably the one used in connection with the sacrifices. Nahmanides' invocation of Kabbalah here as providing the truth (*ha-'emet*) does not mean that he regarded all other interpretations as false. There is a hierarchy of truth, with Kabbalah at the top. Its teaching is that human action here below, when performed properly and with proper intention (*kavvanah*), positively affects the divine life above. By arguing in this vein, Nahmanides raised what seemed a historical contingency in Maimonides to a level vital in the very life of God.

The reasons Nahmanides assigned for the *mishpatim* and *'edot* are usually grounded in human need: Human beings need laws to govern their relationships. Jews need to commemorate the great events when God's power and providence were so unmistakably manifest. But with the *huqqim*, especially the positive precepts of the Temple cult, human need is not the essential teleology at work. Commenting on the verse, "And they shall know that I am the Lord their God, who brought them out of the land of Egypt to dwell (*le-shokhni*) in their midst" (Exodus 29:46), Nahmanides writes:

> There is in this passage a great mystical teaching (*sod gadol*). For according to the ostensible meaning of the text (*ke-fi peshat*) the presence of the *Shekhinah* is a mortal need (*tsorekh hedyot*), not a need of the Supernal (*tsorekh Gavoah*). But the theme is analogous to that of the verse, "O Israel, it is in you whom I glorify myself" (Isaiah 49:3).[73]

Ordinary people, who live basically within the realms of nature and history – realms separate form God's being, although not from God's power – need to see the commandments as fulfilling their ordinary human needs. Extraordinary souls, however, live essentially within the divine life, as the Temple is within the divine life. They need only to see the commandments as fulfilling divine needs, with which they are so intimately involved.

The subject of divine needs engrossed the kabbalists after Nahmanides.[74] Some even saw the emanation of the multifold world from divine oneness as resulting from God's need for an "other."[75] Nahmanides does not seem to intend so radical a suggestion, that creation is not wholly a free act. What his invocation of kabbalistic doctrine seems to mean is that *since* God has chosen to extend himself into mutiplicity, he has *thereby* made himself dependent on it, *insofar* as he is present in it. But, as the wholly transcendent Infinite (*Ayn Sof*), God is never wholly dependent on what participates in his life. For he is never wholly present in it.

In his introduction to the *Commentary on the Torah*, Nahmanides emphatically affirms the kabbalistic dictum that the Torah's sanctity reflects the fact that its words are all permutations of the names of God.[76] Thus God is present in the Torah and in that sense needs it as a person needs any vital organ. But God is always more than his names; indeed *Ayn Sof* (the "In-finite") is a negative term: Essentially God is nameless. At this level, what Nahmanides seems to mean by *divine need* is that by performing the commandments, especially the *huqqim*, at least some Jews are not just passive recipients of God's grace but active participants in the divine life. This aspect of Nahmanides' kabbalistic theology probably had a greater influence on subsequent Kabbalah than any other.[77]

One can always debate the adequacy of Nahmanides' kabbalistic interpretations of the positive *huqqim*, but they frequently offer a richer vein of interpretation than Jewish rationalism had to offer. So it is not hard to see why they were followed up much more thoroughly by later generations than were the rationalist interpretations. But Nahmanides did not limit himself to the positive *huqqim*. The negative *huqqim* also call for interpretation. Maimonides saw these as proscriptions of ancient idolatrous practices. Idolatry itself was the prime human violation of natural law, denying the manifest reality of the transcendent God. Any idolatrous act was in essence a violation of the natural order, an order not invented by human reason but discovered by it. Like the *mishpatim* and the *'edot*, then, the *huqqim* too, for Maimonides, were intelligible ultimately in terms of nature.

For Nahmanides too these prohibitions forbid the violation of an order which is not invented by human reason. But it is not an order which is discovered by human reason either. Rather, the *huqqim* often proscribe violation of the order created by God but discoverable only by revelation. Such laws are fundamentally different from the *mishpatim* or the *'edot*. Their purposes are seen only when something of the created order is revealed to us that is beyond both ordinary human reason and even extraordinary human experience. Commenting on the verse, "You shall keep my statutes (*et huqqotay*): you shall not crossbreed species" (Lev. 19:19), Nahmanides writes:

> The *huqqim* are the decree of the King (*gezerat ha-melekh*), which he decreed (*yihoq*) in his kingdom without revealing their utility (*to'eletam*) to the people... The person who crossbreeds species changes and falsifies the very work of creation, as though he thought that God did not adequately fulfill every need (*she-lo-hishleem kol tsorekh*).[78]

Crossbreeding is, in effect, a denial of the adequacy of creation. It is tampering with the created order, as though God did not satisfactorily finish his work and man could improve upon it. The proscription, then, is for the sake of affirming that God's creation is perfect, although human reason frequently does not understand how God's providence operates in creation and does in fact secure the needs of every creature. Fuller understanding of the ways of providence must await revelation of the sort that Job ultimately received from God.[79]

The prohibition against changing the created order, even to improve it, is in essence a proscription of magic. Maimonides justifies the prohibition of magic not because it is objectively efficacious in disrupting the natural order, but because it is subjectively dangerous.[80] It distorts our understanding of the true operations of nature, which are made out through scientific investigation, not superstitious opinion. Human action cannot alter the settled natural order, let alone affect the transcendent life of God. But for Nahmanides, magic is objectively efficacious. It is proscribed not because belief in it is false, but because it is an evil attempt to manipulate God for human advantage.[81] Such evil can indeed upset the order of creation, perhaps even thwarting temporarily the fulfillment of divine plans. It can never overturn God's sovereignty. But we mortals are forbidden to act as if we had control over God. As Lenn Goodman puts it, magic is proscribed by Nahmanides in much the way that children are forbidden to mock the authority of their parents. Human power is justified (and efficacious) ultimately only when it is a faithful participation in the life of God and his governance of the universe.

6. *The Primacy of Exegesis.*

Nahmanides' writings, especially his *Commentary on the Torah*, voice recurring themes that can be sytematically related. But many readers have failed to grasp his system because they expect a *wholly* kabbalistic system of theology. Not finding that, they often assume that that there is no system at all. Taking at face value Nahmanides' treatment of Kabbalah as the highest truth of the Torah, they assume that he must have regarded it as the sole truth of the Torah. But, as we have seen, he also finds in the Torah a commitment to the reality of nature and history, even if that level of truth is transcended by the Kabbalah. Kabbalah, the highest truth, does not displace all other truths but puts them in perspective. Kabbalah alone does not suffice to explain the Torah. But it is necessary, in Nahmanides' view, to any adequate theology of Judaism.

One cannot be sure why Nahmanides did not develop a more homogenous theology, like that of the *Zohar* and some subsequent kabbalists.[82] He certainly had the intellectual gifts for systematic thinking. But had he presented a strictly kabbalistic theology, the richness of his approach would have been much diminished. His eclecticism allows a diversity of the types and methods of interpretation; and it is primarily as an exegete that he is best understood. A comprehensive system would have narrowed his exegetical options.[83] As an exegete he could find levels of meaning in Scripture which may seem contradictory when arrayed side by side. But for him, evidently, the text addresses different persons in different ways simultaneously. In the end, the richness of the text takes precedence to the abstract elegance of a comprehensive system.

Thus Nahmanides' theology, is more heuristic than constructive. Its purpose seems always to be to explain the text rather than simply to use it to illustrate themes the author brings to it. The fruits of his method provide all Jewish thinkers with a wealth of substantive insights into the Torah and the model of that method itself, a powerful theological hermeneutic. Where Nahmanides is systematic, his system is more hermeneutical than philosophical. In Isaiah Berlin's well known division of thinkers into hedgehogs and foxes: those who relate everything to a single central vision and those who puruse many ends, often unrelated or even contradictory,[84] Nahmanides is more the hedgehog than the fox, a more centrifugal thinker, where, say, Maimonides is more centripetal. The precedence of datum over theory, of exegesis over system is, after all, what makes one a scriptural as opposed to a systematic theologian.

Notes to the Introduction

1 *Rabbi Moses Nahmanides (RAMBAN): Explorations in his Religious and Literary Virtuosity*, 1-2.

2 The following editions of Nahmanides' works were used: *Commentary on the Torah* (CT) 2 vols., ed. C. B. Chavel (Jerusalem: Mosad Harav Kook, 1959-63); *Kitvei Ramban* (KR) 2 vols., ed. Chavel (Jerusalem: Mosad Harav Kook, 1963); *Hidushei ha-Ramban*, 2 vols., ed. I. Z. Meltzer (B'nai B'rak: n.p., 1959); *Hidushei ha-Ramban ha-Shalem*, 4 vols., ed. M. Hershler et al. (Jerusalem: Makhon ha-Talmud ha-Yisraeli, 1970-87); *Notes on Maimonides' Sefer ha-Mitsvot*, ed. Chavel (Jerusalem: Mosad Harav Kook, 1981); *Teshuvot ha-Ramban*, ed. Chavel (Jerusalem: Mosad Harav Kook, 1975).

3 For the effects of reconstructing original texts in a new context, see B. Pesahim 105b and Rashbam, s.v. "*ve-sadrana 'ana.*" For an excellent contemporary example of scholarly and philosophic reconstruction of the thought of a medieval Jewish theologian, see Lenn E. Goodman, ed., *The Book of Theodicy: Translation and Commentary on the Book of Job by Saadiah ben Joseph Al-Fayyumi*.

4 Thus in an 1803 responsum addressing a request for an endorsement of a project of publishing Nahmanides' *Commentary on the Torah*, the Hatam Sofer wrote that "although the books of Nahmanides are to be found, those who engage in the study of them are not to be found." He called the *Commentary on the Torah* "a foundation of faith and a root of religion." *Sefer Hatam Sofer* (New York: n.p., 1958) 6, no. 61.

5 That year culminated in my writing an essay, "Belief in God," later published in my *Law and Theology in Judaism*, ch. 15.

6 An earlier version of this introduction formed my "Nahmanides' Commentary on the Torah," *Solomon Goldman Lectures*, ed. B. L. Sherwin and M. Carasik (Chicago: Spertus College of Judaica Press, 1990) 87-104. Much can still be learned from J. Perles'classic essay, "Über den Geist des Commentar der Rabbi Moses ben Nachman zum Pentateuch," *Monatschrift für Geschichte und Wissenschaft des Judenthums* 8 (1858) 81 ff.

7 Unlike Halakhah, whose prescriptions are transmitted or legislated by the rabbinic authorities of the community for the community (see Maimonides, *Hilkhot Mamrim*, ch. 1), Aggadah is an individual sage's suggestion of what he thinks should be done over and above Halakhah, especially in the area of doctrine, where there are few halakhic rules. Aggadah is normative, not just descriptive (see Y. Megillah 4.1 / 74d), but it is not legally binding (see Y. Peah 2.6 / 10a; Y. Horayot 3.5 / 48c re Eccl. 6:2). Thus it is urged,

"When you desire to know God, study Aggadah" (*Sifre: Devarim*, ed. Finkelstein, no. 49). The quest for God is mandatory, as is clear from the verse on which this text comments: "...which I command you to do: to love the Lord your God, to walk in his ways, and to cleave to him" (Deut. 11:22). See Maimonides, *Shemonah Peraqim*, 5, ad init.

8 The relation of *peshat* (ostensible meaning) and *derash* (explicated meaning) is subtle. Thus the principle, "Scripture speaks of its own present time (*be-hoveh*)," is used to explain why certain things are mentioned in a particular law. But the law is not limited to these cases; rather the items in question are seen as *examples* of a general class which includes a potential infinitude of other cases. Thus, what may seem an assertion of the self sufficiency of *peshat* is actually a basis for *derash*, a search for the principle underlying the examples. See, e.g., M. Baba Kama 5.7; cf. *Encyclopedia Talmudit* **6**.553-55. The rabbinic principle, "Scripture does not depart from its ostensible meaning (*middei peshuto*)" was not understood to foreclose *derash* but to give it a basis. See B. Yevamot 24a and parallels; *Midrash Leqaḥ Tov*: Vayetse, ed. S. Buber, 72b-73a; and David Weiss Halivni, *Peshat and Derash: Plain and Applied Meaning in Rabbinic Exegesis* (New York: Oxford University Press, 1991) 3 ff., 79 ff. On the role of *ta'amei ha-mitsvot* in normative interpretation, see I. Heinemann, *Ta'amei ha-Mitsvot be-Sifrut Yisrael* (Jerusalem: World Zionist Organization, 1949) **1**.11 ff.

9 See R. Israel Meir Ha-Kohen, *Mishnah Berurah* on *Shulhan 'Arukh*: 'Orah Hayyim, 60.4, n. 11.

10 *Kavvanat ha-lev* in this sense originally applied only to the commandment of reciting the first verse of the *Shema* and the *Shemonah Esreh*. See M. Berakhot 2.1; *Sifre Devarim*, no. 41; cf. David Weiss Halivni, *Meqorot u-Mesorot*: Mo'ed (Yoma - Hagigah) (Jerusalem: Jewish Theological Seminary of America, 1975) 404-05. But in time *kavvanat ha-lev* became a desideratum for all *mitsvot*. See esp. Nahmanides, *Notes on Maimonides' Sefer ha-Mitsvot*, pos. no. 5.

11 See *God in Search of Man*, 320 ff. Cf. Bahya ibn Pakuda, *Hovot ha-Levavot*: Sha'ar ha-Ma'aseh, ch. 1 ff.

12 CT: Lev. 19:2/II, 115; cf. CT: Deut. 27:26.

13 See I. Tishby, *Mishnat ha-Zohar*, **2**.387. Martin Buber, in *Two Types of Faith*, 57, holds that *Halakhah* is antithetical to a true I-Thou relationship of man and God; I respond in *Jewish-Christian Dialogue*, 89-91.

14 As precedent for the view that the search for the reasons of the commandments should lead only to better observance of them, not to their neglect, see Philo, *Migration of Abraham*, 89-93.

15 *Moreh Nevukhim*, 3.27.

16 *Moreh*, 3.48. See D. Novak, *Law and Theology in Judaism*, **2**.40 ff.

17 See Maimonides, *Hilkhot Yesodei ha-Torah*, 4.13; *Moreh*, 2.33; cf. Menachem Kellner, *Maimonides on Human Perfection* (Atlanta: Scholars Press, 1990) for an account of Maimonides' conception of the highest kinds of human activity that does not lend itself to such a reductionism — or misappropriation of Maimonides' aims.

18 See *Hilkhot Teshuvah*, 3.4: "Even though sounding the shofar on Rosh Hashanah is a Scriptural decree (*gezerat ha-katuv*), it contains a hint (*remez*) of its intention, namely (*kelomar*): 'Awake you sleepers from your slumber... search your deeds, return in penitence, and remember your Creator!"

19 See J. Sarachek, *Faith and Reason: The Conflict Over the Rationalism of Maimonides* (New York: Hermon, 1970) 75 ff., 84-85, 116 ff.

20 See C. B. Chavel, *Rabbenu Mosheh ben Nahman* (Jersualem: Mosad Harav Kook, 1967) 120 ff.

21 See, e.g., CT: Exod. 20:23. For Nahmanides' classification of the *mitsvot*, C. Henoch, *Ha-Ramban ke-Hoqer u-Mequbbal* (Jerusalem: Harry Fischel Institute, 1978) 337 ff.

22 See, e.g., Solomon Schechter, "Nachmanides," *Studies in Judaism* (New York: Macmillan, 1896) **1**.119-20.

23 See David Berger, "Miracles and the Natural Order in Nahmanides" in Twersky, ed., *Rabbi Moses Nahmanides*, 107 ff.

24 T. Avodah Zarah 8.4; B. Sanhedrin 56a-b.

25 See Saadiah Gaon, *ED*, 9.2 re Gen. 2:16; and my *The Image of the Non-Jew in Judaism*, esp. ch. 10.

26 See Joseph Albo, *Sefer ha-'Iqqarim*, 1.7; also, Novak, *The Image*, ch. 11.

27 *Hilkhot Melakhim*, 8.11.

28 *Shemonah Peraqim*, 6; cf. *Commentary on the Mishnah*, Berakhot 5.3.

29 See Novak, *The Image*, 276 ff.

30 For the need of metaphysics in morality, see *Moreh*, 2.40, 3.27; for the need of metaphysics by morality, 3.54. For the logic of the interdependence, see my "Maimonides' Concept of Practical Reason," *Proceedings of the European Association of Jewish Studies 1990* (forthcoming).

31 CT: Gen. 6:13 - I, 52. Cf. CT: Gen. 6:2. For Nahmanides' use of the term *mitsvot sikhliyot*, see KR: *Commentary on Job*, 1:1, I, 26; *Torat ha-Shem Temimah*, KR I, 173.

32 CT: Exod. 12:21 1.334.28. For a possibly similar view in Maimonides (*Hilkhot Yesodei ha-Torah*, 7.5), see my *Jewish-Christian Dialogue*, 129 ff.

33 "The custom operates before we have time for reflexion... much more without forming any principle concerning it, or reasoning upon that principle." David Hume, *A Treatise of Human Nature*, 1.3.8, ed. L. A. Selby-Bigge (Oxford: Clarendon Press, 1888) 104. For the Islamic background, see L. E. Goodman, "Did al-Ghazâlî Deny Causality," *Studia Islamica* 47 (1978) 83-120.

34 See, e.g., CT: Deut. 13:2.

35 CT: Exod. 13:16 - I, 346.

36 See W. H. Walsh, *An Introduction to Philosophy of History* (London: Hutchinson, 1967) 63 ff.

37 See Mircea Eliade, *The Sacred and the Profane: The Nature of Religion* (New York: Harper and Row, 1961) 106-07.

38 See CT: Gen. 14:10; and Y. Silman's excellent treatment of Halevi's views on revelation and history, *Bayn Filosof le-Navi* (Ramat-Gan: Bar-Ilan University Press, 1985) 161 ff., 216 ff.

39 CT: Gen. 22:1, I - 125-26.

40 For this twofold teleology of the *mitsvot*, see CT: Deut.22:6.

41 See CT: Deut. 11:22.

42 *Bemidbar Rabbah* 19.1; cf. *Midrash Leqah Tov*: Huqqat, 119b.

43 *Bereshit Rabbah* 44.1 and parallels; cf. Maimonides' handling of this rabbinic text at *Moreh*, 3.26.

44 *Sifra*: Aharei Mot, ed. Weiss, 86a; B. Yoma 67b. For further elaborations of this *"facio quia absurdum"* theme in medieval Ashkenazic theology, see D. Berger, *Jewish-Christian Debate* (Philadelphia: JPS, 1979) 356-57.

45 See my "Natural Law, Halakhah and the Covenant", *JLA* 7 (1988) 47 ff.

46 See *Hilkhot Talmud Torah*, 1.11-12; *Moreh*, Introduction.

47 *Moreh*, 3.43.

[48] See D. Novak, "Does Maimonides have a Philosophy of History?" in Samuelson, ed., *Studies in Jewish Philosophy*; Henoch, *Ramban*, 316-17.

[49] See, especially, *Moreh* 2.31. The Talmudic Rabbis, by contrast, stressed the uniquely Jewish meaning of the Sabbath. See B. Sanhedrin 58b re Gen. 8:22; *Devarim Rabbah* 1.18 re Exod. 31:17.

[50] *Moreh*, 3.37.

[51] *Moreh*, 3.48. See *Hilkhot Ma'akhalot Assurot*, 17.29-31; also, *Hilkhot De'ot*, 3.3 re Mishnah Avot 2.2.

[52] See, e.g., *Moreh*, 1.36; 3.29.

[53] See, e.g., J. Even-Chen, *Ha-Ramban* (Jerusalem: Ginzekha Rishonim Le-Tsiyon, 1976) 61 ff. The notion that Nahmanides had a complete, largely secret kabbalistic system was apparently held even by his contemporaries who found his kabbalism excessive. See R. Isaac bar Sheshet Parfat, *Teshuvot ha-Ribash*, no. 157. For modern critical discussion of Nahmanides' kabbalism, see Gershom Scholem, *Ha-Kabbalah be-Gerona*, 73 ff., and *Origins of the Kabbalah*, 384; M. Idel, *Kabbalah: New Perspectives*, 254.

[54] See *Major Trends in Jewish Mysticism*, 173.

[55] See M. Idel, "We Have No Kabbalistic Tradition on This" in Twersky, ed., *Rabbi Moses Nahmanides*, 63 ff.

[56] See Scholem, *Ha-Kabbalah be-Gerona*, 66; Idel, *Kabbalah: New Perspectives*, 215.

[57] See, e.g., *Zohar*: Aharei-Mot, 3:73a.

[58] See Saadiah Gaon, *ED*, 1.2, 4.

[59] See Gershom Scholem, *On the Kabbalah and Its Symbolism*, 145; *Major Trends in Jewish Mysticism*, 177-78.

[60] *Zohar*: Bereshit, 1:36a. See Menahem Recanti, *Commentary on the Torah*: Gen. 2:16 and 8:21; Novak, *The Image*, 267-68. Rationalistic and kabbalistic approaches to the Noahide laws are combined in Judah Loewe (Maharal), *Gevurot ha-Shem* (Cracow, 1582) ch. 66.

[61] Cf. Gershom Scholem, "Schöpfung aus Nichts und Selbstverschränkung Gottes," *Eranos Jahrbuch* 25 (1956) 108 ff.

[62] Following the Halevian/Nahmanidean view of history, Judah Loewe (Maharal) distinguishes between physical time (*zeman*) and historical time (*sha'ah, rega'*). See *Gevurot ha-Shem*, sec. 2. Cf. L. E. Goodman, "Time,

Creation and the Mirror of Narcissus," *Philosophy East and West* 42 (1992).

63 See *Kuzari*, 1.67; 5.20.

64 See Novak, *Jewish-Christian Dialogue*, 142 ff.

65 See *Torat ha-Adam*: Sha'ar ha-Gemul / KR II, 302. Cf. Maimonides, *Hilkhot Teshuvah*, 8.8 and Rabad's note ad loc.

66 See, e.g., CT: Num. 1:45 re B. Pesahim 64b.

67 See, e.g., Menahem Recanti, *Commentary on the Torah*: Exod. 29:1 and Lev. 26:3 (Venice, 1523), where he speaks of the"natural" (= necessary) causality of the commandments (*teva kol mitsvah u-mitsvah*), i.e., in the true divine realm, not the illusory, separated physical realm. Also, see his comment on Exod. 34:6, where transitive divine acts become inner divine properties (cf. B. Shabbat 133b). For the same idea of divine nature in the thought of a modern Jewish mystic deeply indebted to the Kabbalah, see Abraham Isaac Kook, *'Orot Ha-Qodesh*, ed. D. Cohen (Jerusalem: Mosad Harav Kook, 1963) I, 143-44. Further, see Scholem, *Origins of the Kabbalah*, 453; also, Berger, "Miracles and the Natural Order in Nahmanides," 121. Cf. Idel, *Kabbalah: New Perspectives*, 102.

68 See Tishby, *Mishnat ha-Zohar* **1**.3 ff.

69 See Tishby, **1**.287 ff.

70 See his "Introduction to Notes on the Enumeration of the Commandments", KR I, 420; also, Scholem, *Origins of the Kabbalah*, 389.

71 CT: Lev. 1:9 - II, 11 re *Moreh Nevukhim* 3.46. See *Targum Onkelos*, Gen. 43:32; Ibn Ezra, *Commentary on the Torah*, Exod. 8:22.

72 Re B. Shabbat 87a and B. Hagigah 14a. See *Zohar*: Vayiqra, 3:9b.

73 CT: Exod. 29:46 - I, 486-87.

74 See, e.g., Meir ibn Gabbai, *Avodat ha-Qodesh*, 2.2 ff. For the contrary view of most Talmudic rabbis, see, e.g., Y. Nedarim 9.1/41b re Job 35:7; and Saadiah Gaon, *Emunot ve-De'ot*, 3.10. But, cf. B. Berakhot 7a; B. Baba Metsia 114a re Deut. 8:10.

75 See, e.g., Hayyim Vital, *'Ets Hayyim*, 1:11a.

76 Chavel, following the traditionalist view that the *Zohar* is a source for Nahmanides, sees the source (*meqoro*) of this doctrine in the *Zohar*: Yitro, 2:87a (see CT, introduction, ed. Chavel, 6, note). More plausibly, Nahmanides was the *Zohar*'s source for this basic kabbalistic doctrine.

One application of the theological point is in grounding the halakhic norm that a *Sefer Torah* defective in any way is ritually invalid for the public reading in the synagogue (Maimonides, *Hilkhot Sefer Torah*, 10.1, nos.12 and 13), see Abraham ben Yom Tov Ishbili, *Teshuvot ha-Ritba*, ed. Kafih (Jerusalem: Mosad Harav Kook, 1959), no. 142, pp. 167-70. The Ritba cites Nahmanides, not the *Zohar*, as the *locus classicus* for this point. For doubts as to the antiquity of the *Zohar* by a premodern traditionalist scholar, see Jacob Emden, *Mitpahat Sefarim* (Altona, 1769); cf. Scholem, *Major Trends*, 181.

77 A profound restatement of the kabbalistic doctrine of the interaction of divine and human needs was made by Abraham Joshua Heschel in *Man Is Not Alone*, 241 ff.

78 CT: Lev. 19:19/ II, 120. See, also, CT: Lev. 26:15.

79 See Nahmanides' *Commentary on Job*, 42:5 - KR I, 126.

80 See *Hilkhot Avodah Zarah*, 11.16; *Commentary on the Mishnah*: Pesahim 4.10.

81 See, e.g., CT: Exod. 8:14.

82 See Scholem, *Origins of Kabbalah*, 384; Bernard Septimus, "Nahmanides and the Andalusian Tradition" in Twersky, ed., *Rabbi Moses Nahmanides*, 19 ff.; E. R. Wolfson, "By Way of Truth," 125-29, 163-76.

83 For Nahmanides' thesis that a commandment can have more than one reason, see CT: Exod. 20:23; cf. B. Sanhedrin 34a re Jer. 23:29; Bemidbar Rabbah 13.15.

84 Isaiah Berlin, *The Hedgehog and the Fox* (New York: Simon and Schuster, 1953) 1.

Chapter 1

The Human Soul

[1.1] The human soul is the locus of the immediate knowledge of God, because it is not part of the created physical order. Thus it is capable of more than just experience of the world.

> The virtue or excellence of the soul (*ma'alat ha-nefesh*), its source and its mystery... it did not come from the physical elements or by mediation of the disembodied intelligences. Rather, it is the spirit of the Great Name, from his mouth, knowledge and understanding. For it is from the foundation of Understanding (*binah*), by way of Truth and Faith (*emet ve-'emunah*). [CT: Gen. 2:7 - I, 33]

This passage is replete with allusions to the *sefirot*, the supernal manifestations of the Godhead, which were elaborately and precisely mapped by later kabbalists. But the central point is that the soul is no mere created entity but a direct emanation from the Godhead.

[1.2] As a composite of soul and body, a human being is in direct relationship with both God and nature. No adequate understanding of the human condition can ignore our compositeness. Nahmanides elicits this point from the use of the plural in the creation narrative of Genesis 1, where God says, "let us make (*na'aseh*) man":

> Man's... nature is not like that of a beast. "In our image, according to our likeness" means that he resembles both... earthly beings (*tahtonim*) and higher, angelic beings (*'elyonim*). [CT: Gen. 1:26 - I, 27]

Although Nahmanides cites only the view of Joseph Kimhi (ca. 1150), rabbinic precedent too can be found for this theological anthropology, in *Avot de-Rabbi Nathan* (A, ed. Schechter, 55a; B. Ta'anit 16a). Unlike Maimonides (*Moreh Nevukhim*, 2.5-6), Nahmanides distinguishes the intelligent heavenly bodies from the higher angelic beings. That the angels are greater grows more evident in the sections immediately following.

[1.3] It is only the relationship with God that differentiates man from the beasts. Commenting on Kohelet's dismissal of the distinction between man and beast, Nahmanides writes:

> This is astounding! How can it be that "man's preeminence over a beast is naught" (Eccl. 3:19)? Are there not humans who reach so high a level as to be covenanted with God, beloved of God like Abraham, rejoiced in like Jacob? But the intent of the verse is that by our own deeds we have no preeminence, and that no human being has the power to make his body greater than that of a beast. Yet we have the power to do the will of our Creator, to cleave to him, as the patriarchs did, who enjoyed exceptional intimacy with God, and heightened virtue (*ma'alah yeteirah*), and whose name and memory remains in this world even now for the generations of their descendants. [KR: *Sermon on Ecclesiastes* - I, 193]

[1.4] The duality of our nature explains the tensions inherent in the human condition:

> Man... was to be like the ministering angels in his soul... but he was drawn in the direction of the flesh because he is carnal, not godly. [CT: Gen. 6:3 - I, 49]

Even more pointedly:

> The root of man's suffering in the world of bodies is that man's body is like the body of an animal, produced under the influence of the stars and constellations, thus subject to vicissitudes. Only the soul is from God who gave it. [KR: *Commentary on Job* 22:2 - I, 76]

For Nahmanides, both natural and moral evil arise in our embodiment. But natural evil seems necessary, whereas moral evil stems from our own volitions. Yet so does our potential for transcendence. Human beings who find their true selves in the soul rather than the body can even overcome many of the vicissitudes to which our embodiment renders us vulnerable.

[1.5] In the souls of the righteous, the spiritual dimension is more pronounced:

> In the tradition of the Rabbis of blessed memory, God created the souls of the righteous; and, without doubt, the soul is an exceedingly fine and pure spirit. It is not a body and not confined to a place... but it comes from the category (*kat*) of the angels and is exceedingly exalted. [KR: *Torat ha-'Adam*: Sha'ar ha-Gemul - II, 285]

[1.6] The souls of the righteous all stem from the very source and origin of creation. Nahmanides here affirms the primordial existence of human souls:

> Those who err spiritually think that souls are created every day, each with its own storehouse [the body]. But that is not so. For God does not create them *ex nihilo*. The higher beings (*ha-'elyonim*) were created from the very beginning before all else (*me'az*). The lower beings (*ha-shefalim*), which come to be and pass away are made one from another, altering and assuming forms. [KR: *Commentary on Job* 38:21 - I, 117-118]

[1.7] Since the human soul is an immediate creation of God, it presupposes nothing else:

> For generation is by the blessing of God. For souls are not born but were created from nothing (*me-'ayin*). [CT: Gen. 5:2 - I, 47]

Elsewhere, he elaborates:

> The correct and clear interpretation of this section [the creation narrative of Genesis 1] is that God did not create everything *ex nihilo* on those days, but only the primary substances (*ha-hiyulim*) mentioned... But regarding the creation of man he stated... [as it were] "I and the earth"... for the body is earthly in form and likeness in that it is mortal and perishes, but the soul (*nefesh*) is in a higher form (*tselem*), which is not corporeal and over which coming-to-be (*ha-havayah*) and perishing have no dominion. [KR: *Torat ha-Shem Temimah* - I, 157-158]

[1.8] An immediate divine creation, the human soul can be augmented by God in a subsequent act of creation. Commenting on the traditional play on words which finds in Scripture an apparent reference to ensoulment on or of the Sabbath (*vayinafash*, Exod. 31:17), Nahmanides, following the

Talmud [B. Betsah 16a], locates the ensoulment in the Jew who observes the Sabbath and thereby receives an "additional soul" (*nefesh yeterah*):

> The additional soul comes from the foundation (*yesod*) of the world. [CT: Exod. 32:13 - I, 505]

Yesod is the ninth of the ten *sefirot*. Nahmanides' use of this kabbalistic language underscores the emanative origin of the soul. It is not produced like some material object.

[1.9] The function of the body is to serve the soul. For the soul performs its obligations by means of the body. The death of the body is to be mourned as the loss of the outward capacity to fulfill the commandments:

> It seems to me that the soul functions in the body as the names of God function on the parchment of a Torah scroll... One might also say that as one rends his clothes when a Torah scroll is burned [B. Mo'ed Qatan 25a], so should one rend his clothes when those who uphold the commandments die... for with their death the performance of positive commandments is diminished. Thus everyone should rend his clothes at the death of any Jew, even a woman. [KR: *Torat ha-'Adam* - II, 52]

[1.10] Only human beings have immortal rational souls, but even the higher animals have souls in the sense of a life principle or vital spirit. Thus they are not to be exploited without limitation:

> The souls of those creatures with an animal soul (*nefesh ha-tenu'ah*) have a certain elevated standing, whereby they resemble creatures with rational souls (*ha-nefesh ha-maskelet*)... God gave human beings permission (*reshut*) to slaughter and eat them, since they exsist for the sake of humans. But he did not permit us to eat their soul, that is, their blood. [CT: Gen. 1:29 - I, 29]

In Scripture, the vital soul of an animal is its blood and the force it embodies. That blood is offered back to God (Gen. 9:4; Deut. 12:23-25). Vegetative life and minerals, however, do not have souls even in this limited sense; hence, they may be used unreservedly.

[1.11] Animals remain subordinate to human purposes, not least in matters of religion. For their blood plays an important role in the sacrificial cult. For Nahmanides, sacrifice serves not only human needs like that of expiating sin, but it also allows participation in the divine life itself:

> It is not right to mingle the mortal soul (*ha-nefesh ha-nikhretet*) with the immortal soul (*ha-nefesh ha-qayyemet*), but it is to be an atonement on the altar, to be pleasing before the Lord. [CT: Lev. 17:11 - II, 95]

[1.12] The distinction between the human soul and that of the higher beasts is that the beast's

> spirit is from the elements (*ha-yesodot*), but man's body will separate from his soul. [CT: Gen. 1:20 - I, 25]

The term for soul (*nefesh*) seems to be used interchangably in Scripture both for human and animal life (see, e.g., Gen. 1:24, 2:7). But Nahmanides makes a careful distinction between the vital but mortal soul of animals and the rational and immortal soul of human beings.

Chapter 2

Faith

[2.1] What distinguishes the human person is the capacity for conscious relationship with God. Nahmanides calls the human side of this relationship *emunah*, faith or certitude. His central task as a theologian is to relate the human desire for such consciousness with revealed truth, *emet*. Our exercise of faith is the very purpose of creation; it grounds all God's relations with nature:

> The Lord created all lower creatures for man's sake, for man is the only one of them who recognizes (*makir*) his Creator. [CT: Lev. 17:11 - II, 97]

[2.2] Without conscious relationship with God, human existence is pointless. And since the rest of creation exists for the sake of humanity, without our acknowledgement of God, all existence would be pointless.

> There is no [intrinsic] reason (*ta'am*) for the formation of lower animals and plants, for they do not recognize their Creator; only man does. God created man to acknowledge (*makir*) his Creator, may he be exalted. If man had no awareness at all that God created him – all the more if he did not know that for his Creator there are favored and desirable acts and other acts that are undesirable and vile – man would be like a beast, and the object of creation would be vitiated (*betelah*)... The very purpose of the creation of the world would be made void. [KR: *Torat ha-Shem Temimah* - I, 142-43]

Spelling out that purpose, Nahmanides writes:

> It is the intent (*kavvanah*) of the creation (*yetsirah*) of humans. For there is no other reason (*ta'am*) for the formation of man, and God has no desire for lower beings (*tahtonim*) except that man should know and acknowledge the God who created him. This is the reason for raising one's voice in synagogues, and this is the merit of public prayer, that humans have a place in which they gather to acknowledge the God who created them and brought them into existence, so that they should say, "We are your creatures!" [*Ibid.* - I, 152-53]

[2.3] All sublunar creation is for the sake of man:

> So now does Elihu continue in the way of the other friends, relating God's praises and his providence over the world. For he guards his world and watches over it continually... it is impossible to believe that there is no providence even over the least of human beings... for the lower creatures were created for man's sake, since as none but man recognizes its Creator. If all God's care and protection of lower species is for the sake of man, how could he not exercise providential care over man himself? [KR: *Commentary on Job* 36:2 - I, 107-08]

Nahmanides differs sharply here from Maimonides (*Moreh Nevukhim*, 3.13), who set the non-physical heavenly intelligences, identified with the angels (*Moreh*, 2.5-6), higher than man in the created order, because they are not plagued by the uncertainties of volition (*Moreh*, 1.2; 3.17). Man relates to God through this higher, intellectual nature of the angels, aspiring to be as much like it as possible. For Nahmanides, the angels are higher than the heavenly bodies, and so is man (CT: Gen. 2:7 - I, 33). Thus man, like the angels, can relate to God, by transcending nature, both earthly and celestial.

[2.4] Because God's relationship with human souls is direct, it is individual. But God's relation to the rest of creation is only specific and indirect:

> Nowhere in the Torah or the prophets is it ever claimed that God's providence superintends (*mashgiah*) individual members of inarticulate species. In their case providence extends only to the species, which are in the same category as the heavens and their structures. Thus the slaughter (*shehitah*) of animals was permitted to meet human needs, and also to atone for our lives through their blood on the altar. The reason for this is clear and obvious. It is because man recognizes his God as the one who cares for him and watches over him. [KR: *Commentary on Job* 36:7 - I, 108]

[2.5] By emphasizing the immediacy of the soul's relationship with God, Nahmanides stakes out a position markedly different from the whole project of rationalist Jewish theology from Saadiah to Maimonides. Such theology was based on the idea that one could trace a path from knowledge of the world to God as its necessary cause. Nahmanides did not deny the legitimacy of such an inference. But he saw it as an insufficient basis for the relationship between God and man. Positive knowledge of God must come from God himself to be worthy of its object.

Commenting on Moses' request at the Burning Bush that God reveal his proper name, Nahmanides engages in a pointed polemic with rationalist Jewish theology from Saadiah to Maimonides and beyond. As in virtually all such polemics on his part, he aims both at what he takes to be a faulty exegesis of the text and at what he takes to be the faulty theology behind it.

> He asked him his name so that the Lord might tell it, giving them [the Israelites] perfect instruction about his existence and providence... According to Saadiah Gaon... and Maimonides... we must infer that God told Moses... that he should give them specific rational proofs (*r'ayot sikhliyot*) whereby his name would be accepted by the wise... But this is not the meaning of the verse. The mention of the Name to them *is* the proof. This is the sign and demonstration in answer to what they would ask. [CT: Exod. 3:13 - I, 292]

In other words, God's answer, literally, "I shall be who I shall be," is not a conclusion inferred from prior premises. It is God's promise of his own self-presentation to the people of Israel in Egyptian slavery. That is what the Name (the tetragrammaton) signifies. The rabbinic precedents (B. Berakhot 9b and *Shemot Rabbah* 3.6) are cited by Nahmanides.

Much the same point is made in modern Jewish theology by Martin Buber in *Zur einer neuen Verdeutschung der Schrift* (Olten: Jakob Hegner, 1954) 28-29; *Königtum Gottes*, 3rd rev. ed. (Heidelberg: Lambert Schnieder, 1956) 69; and by Franz Rosenzweig, *Kleinere Schriften* (Berlin: Schocken, 1937) 185 ff. See also their joint Pentateuch translation, *Die Fünf Bücher der Weisung* (Olten: Jakob Hegner, 1954) 158 ad Exod. 3:13. But Buber especially confines God's being to his relationality as the Eternal Thou, as we see in *I and Thou* (tr. Kaufmann, 157 ff.) The kabbalistic element in Nahmanides' theology does not allow him to confine God's being (expressed in the tetragrammaton, YHWH) to his relationality. Thus in Nahmanides the importance of the Name is not just in designating divine self-presentation, but in its role in the inner divine life within the *sefirot*. For an attempt at a kabbalistically influenced synthesis of the rabbinic and philosophic readings of the verse, see my article, "Buber and Tillich," (*Journal of Ecumenical Studies*, forthcoming).

[2.6] For Nahmanides, as for most Jewish thinkers, faith is not a matter of belief. That is, it is not an affirmation of what is unknown (cf. Plato, *Republic* 534A). Rather, faith is certitude of what one does know, in this case from intimate experience of God's working in the world. Thus Nahmanides' differences with the rationalist theologians are not a matter of his opposing faith to knowledge but of his insistence that we gain certitude from historical experience without need of a mediating, metaphysical understanding of nature.

Thus, in his account of the disputation at Barcelona, Nahmanides tells of his response to his Christian adversary's references to faith:

> I stood up and said, "it is clear that a person does not have faith in what he does not know." [KR: *Disputation*, no. 107 - I, 320]

Nahmanides contrasts his Jewish view of faith with the Christian view represented in such New Testament passages as 2 Cor. 5:7 and Heb. 11:1, where faith acquires the character of a mystery.

It is always problematic to cite the *Disputation* as an expression of Nahmanides' theological views, since it often seems to exaggerate for rhetorical effect. Yet Nahmanides' claim about faith and knowledge is typical of what might be called his historical empiricism. His approach here is influenced by Halevi, who speaks of "the whole of Israel, who knew these things first from personal experience and afterwards through uninterrupted tradition, which is equal to the former." (*Kuzari*, 1.25, tr. Hirschfeld, 47; cf. 5.14, ad fin.)

The sixteenth century Italian commentator, Judah Moscato (*Qol Yehudah, ad loc.*) marks the powerful influence of Halevi on Nahmanides, citing Nahmanides' reading of Deuteronomy 4:9 (CT: II, 362). He also links the approach with that of Saadiah Gaon. But in my view this latter connection is not as close. Saadiah does not regard the historically transmitted experience conveyed in tradition as a source of knowledge equal to that derived from the senses, intellectual intuition, or logical inference, the three sources of direct knowledge for him (*ED*, 1.5). He holds that tradition is "based upon the knowledge of the senses as well as that of reason" and "corroborates for us the validity of the first three sources of knowledge" (tr. Rosenblatt, 18). In 3.1 (p. 138), Saadiah treats even extraordinary experience (which tradition records and transmits) as only provisional. For in explaining the miracles that accompanied the revelation of the commandments, he writes: "Afterwards we discovered the rational basis for the necessity of their prescription."

For Saadiah, the Torah ultimately expresses the truth of nature, which in principle is accessible to all rational human beings (see L. E. Goodman's note in *The Book of Theodicy: Saadiah's Translation and Commentary on the Book of Job*, 134, n. 13). But in the view that Nahmanides shares with

Halevi, tradition preserves and continues the historical experience of God's direct presence. This experience is not accessible to all but only to the people to whom God has chosen to reveal himself. Indeed, tradition and the revelation it records are the *only* real knowledge of God possible for anyone. This entails an essential difference between traditions that bear the imprint of revelation and those that simply convey or confirm ordinary experiences. Ordinary traditions, like those of conventional history, provide knowledge of what is, at least in principle, more directly available through the senses and reasoning. But traditions that preserve the experience of revelation provide knowledge nowhere else available.

[2.7] Nahmanides recognizes a natural, if indirect, knowledge of God in our awareness of the wonderful workings of the natural order. That awareness can give us the sense that a supernatural direction of the visible world is evident. But such knowledge is a *via negativa*: All that we can infer from it is that the true intelligibility of the world lies beyond our ken. Through revelation, by contrast, we can know the real state of our relationship with the Creator.

> Everything that appears in the world is twofold, containing manifest wisdom (*hokhmah nigleit*) and invisible wisdom (*hokhmah ne'elemet*). In other words, God's providence over creatures is good both explicitly and implicitly. For his good rulership is manifest in the world, and it is known that there is more good than our intellect can grasp. But you do not know and cannot discover for yourself whether you are righteous before God. You can know that only through revealed truth. [KR: *Commentary on Job* 11:6 - I, 53; see 12:3 - I, 54]

The passage echoes the opening of Halevi's *Kuzari*, where the pagan king of the Khazars, himself a philosopher, is told in his dream by an angel: "Thy way of thinking is indeed pleasing to the Creator, but not thy way of acting" (p. 35). This dream is what leads him to seek a better way of life and ultimately to convert to Judaism. The role of philosophy here, understood in the medieval sense as including natural science, is to indicate the existence of God but at the same time to show us that we cannot possibly please God based on what we are capable of learning on our own. The contrast with Saadiah's views is striking. Not only does Saadiah think that all God's commandments are amenable to human reason, but he also assumes, as in the case of Job, that a righteous individual can know with confidence that he has done no wrong. See Saadiah's *Book of Theodicy* (tr. Goodman, 128 and n. 46; cf. 292 n. 10).

[2.8] Thus the indirect revelation of metaphysical reason arouses in us the appetite for the direct revelation of the Torah.

> This is what our sages, of blessed memory, meant when they said [B. Shabbat 88a] that if Israel had not accepted the Torah, God would have returned the universe to chaos: if they had not yearned (*hafetsim*) to know of their Creator and to learn that there is a difference between good and evil, the purpose of creation would be nullifed (*betelah*). [KR: *Torat ha-Shem Temimah* - I, 143]

[2.9] Nahmanides' preference for experience over reason as the basis of our connection with God helps to explain his favoring the Talmudic opinion that the liturgical declaration of the Exodus from Egypt is a Scriptural commandment, whereas the liturgical declaration of the more abstract formula "Hear O Israel, the Lord is our God, the Lord alone" (Deut. 6:4) is only a rabbinic decree (See B. Baba Kama 87a, Tos., s.v. *ve-khen*). Nahmanides is followed in this conclusion by his most important disciple, Solomon ibn Adret, *Responsa Rashba*, 1, no. 329. But neither the Talmudic precedent nor the concurring opinion develops the point theologically as Nahmanides does. For Maimonides, predictably, the preference goes to the more metaphysical formula as the Scripturally mandated recitation (*Sefer ha-Mitsvot*, positive commandments, 10). Nahmanides writes:

> It is, as the rabbis said [B. Berakhot 21a], that the recitation of the *Shema'* is a rabbinic obligation. But the prayer which follows it, "true and certain" (*'emet ve-yatziv*) is Scripturally mandated because it mentions the Exodus from Egypt. [KR: *Torat ha-Shem Temimah* - I, 151]

[2.10] Without the revelation of God's Name, God's self-proclamation, one is left with the "God of the philosophers," but not the God of Abraham, Isaac and Jacob, as Pascal would put it.

In a striking comment, Nahmanides points out that the struggle between Moses and Pharaoh is not a conflict between a theist and an atheist, but between one who knows an actively present God and one who acknowledges a god who is absent, a god whose authority now rests essentially in human hands. Pharaoh's knows his god by an inference from the study of nature. Moses' personal God is directly encountered. Thus Pharaoh's acknowledgment of his god is impersonal and abstract (see CT: Exod. 8:15, I, 312-13, following Ibn Ezra; cf. Rashi *ad loc.*):

> Pharaoh was a very wise man and knew the Divine (*ha-'Elohim*) and acknowledged him... but he did not know the Lord by his unique Name (*ha-shem ha-meyuhad*) and therefore answered "I do not know the Lord". [CT: Exod. 5:3 - I, 300]

[2.11] Commenting on the nineteenth Psalm, where the psalmist affirms, "the heavens declare the glory of God" (19:2) and later, "the Torah of the Lord is perfect, restoring the soul" (19:8), Nahmanides reasons that the knowledge supplied by the Torah is far superior to that achieved through astronomy:

> These are clear proofs of the glory of God, but they are all still the work of his hands. The complete Torah of the Lord, however, is greater than this. It restores the soul and makes the simple wise, because it removes all doubts from the heart, for the wise as well as those who do not know cosmology and astronomy. [KR: *Torat ha-Shem Temimah* - I, 141]

Expanding on the superiority of the revealed Torah to natural theology, Nahmanides writes:

> It is written, "The Torah of the Lord is perfect restoring the soul; the testimony of the Lord is sure making wise the simple" (Ps. 19:8). After stating, "the heavens declare the glory of God" (19:2), he comes back to the merits of the Torah, and states that it declares God's praise (*shevah*) more than the heavens – the sun, moon and stars, which were mentioned above in this psalm. The explanation of this procedure is that David began by stating that the heavens declare the praise of God, because the movement of the heavens is perpetual and unending. Since every movement requires a mover, the heavens affirm the glory of God... these things are clear proofs of the glory of God, for all of them are the work of his hands. But the Torah of the Lord is much more perfect (*shlemah yoter*) . . . it removes all doubts from the hearts of both the learned (*ha-hakhamim*) and those who do not understand the laws of the heavens and the formations of the stars. [*Ibid.* - I, 141]

Maimonides (*Moreh Nevukhim*, 2.5) interprets the psalm much more literally, arguing that the intelligence of the heavenly spheres is the prime indication of God as the ultimate object of their intelligent desire. See also, *Hilkhot Yesodei ha-Torah*, 2.8; 3.9.

[2.12] Revelation can take precedence to independent reason for Nahmanides primarily because of his basic principle that the Torah is prior to creation. He holds this view in a more radical form than do the Rabbis. For them, *both* the Torah and the world are created, but the Torah is prior to the world in the order of creation, temporally or teleologically (B. Pesahim 54a; Bereshit Rabbah 1.1; R. Jacob ibn Habib, *'Ein Ya'aqov*, intro.; H. A. Wolfson, *Repercussions of the Kalam in Jewish Philosophy* [Cambridge: Harvard University Press 1979], 85 ff.).

In Nahmanides' theology the Torah is prior to creation absolutely. It is a direct emanation *of* God, not a separate creation. Thus it is prior to creation as emanation (*atsilut*) is prior to creation (*beri'ah*), a point much developed in the kabbalistic theology that Nahmanides so fundamentally stimulated and influenced. See Tishby, *Mishnat ha-Zohar*, **1**.381 ff.

Essentially different entities require essentially different methods of understanding (see Aristotle, *Nicomachaean Ethics*, 1094b 12-28). Our means of understanding nature are inadequate for understanding the Torah, and, any simlarities are superficial. For the Torah reveals the truth of emanation, a reality prior to creation. It also reveals the truth of creation far more profoundly than unaided human reason can.

In Maimonides' theology the Torah is a created entity, separate from God (*Moreh Nevukhim*, 1.65): "It was ascribed to Him only because the words heard by Moses were created and brought into being by God, just as He created all the things that He created and brought into being" (tr. after Pines, 160). Accordingly, the scientific method applied to nature and adequate to its truth would be adequate to the Torah as well. The truth is to be heard from *whoever* has rationally demonstrated it – even from a (pagan) Greek philosopher like Aristotle (see *Shemonah Peraqim*, introduction; *Moreh*, introduction). Although Greek philosophers did not uncover truths of the Torah as such, they did uncover truths of nature. And both truths are one, substantially and methodologically; they are members of the same genus. The Torah, moreover, like any other natural datum, admits of understanding only by way of science. It does not supply any privileged method of understanding itself or the rest of creation (see *Moreh*, 2.25; *Teshuvot ha-Rambam*, ed. Blau [Jerusalem: Meqitsei Nirdamim, 1960] **2** no. 82). Any contrary claim for the Torah would be superstition (*Commentary on the Mishnah*: Pesahim 4.9).

Because the Torah is created for Maimonides, and because creation is more indirect than emanation, it follows that the mediating role of the historical Moses is much more important for Maimonides than for Nahmanides. Thus Nahmanides writes:

> It would seem that it should have been written at the beginning of the Torah, "And God spoke all these things to Moses, saying–" [Exod. 20:1]. But it had to be written in a more absolute style (*stam*). For Moses did not write the Torah like someone speaking in the first person, as did the other prophets, who did speak in the first person... The reason (*ha-ta'am*) for the Torah's being written in this mode is that it is prior to (*she-qadmah*) the creation of the world... Moreover, we have an authentic tradition (*qabbalah shel emet*) that the whole Torah consists of the names of God – that all the letters could be those names, if so rearranged. [CT: intro. - I, 4, 6]

Later kabbalists laid great emphasis on the difference between second and third person references to God. The third person signifies a higher level of transcendence, since it does not intend anything outside the divine reality itself. A second person statement, by contrast, necessarily intends someone external to the speaker (see *Zohar*: Va-yetse, 156b and 158b; Joseph Gikatila, *Sha'aray 'Orah*, secs. 5, 10; Menahem Recanti, *Commentary on the Torah*: Exod.15:26). Such distinctions were crucial for the kabbalists, since they were convinced that the Torah embodies a science of divine Being, which is ultimately beyond personal reference.

[2.13] The Torah, as the eternal archetype, includes all wisdom:

> Everything is learned from the Torah. God gave King Solomon, peace be upon him, "wisdom and knowledge" (*ha-hokhmah ve-ha-madda* – I Chron. 1:12). All this was his from the Torah. From it he learned the mystery (*sod*) of all natural generation, including the powers of the herbs and their distinctive properties (*segulatam*), so that he could write a medical treatise (*sefer refu'ot*) about them. [CT: Intro. - I,5]

Sefer Refu'ot here means a scientific treatise, a Materia Medica; see Maimonides, *Commentary on the Mishnah*: Pesahim 4.10.

[2.14] The revelation at Sinai is the epitome of the direct encounter between God and man and the paradigm for all such experiences. Hence, such experiences are authentic only when they are subordinate to it.

> We know from the revelation at Mount Sinai, which was face-to-face, that he commanded us to walk in this way, not to serve anyone else whatever. [CT: Deut. 13:2 - II, 405-06]

[2.15] Sinai is the true locus of the tradition. It is the prime experience of God's presence and the source of all genuine human authority in Israel.

> They and their leaders accepted the kingship of God from the utterance of God himself (*mi-pi ha-Gevurah*)... and the Torah, they accepted from the words of Moses. They took it upon themselves and their progeny to believe him [Moses] and to do as he would command them, on the authority of what the King said. [CT: Deut. 33:5 - II, 493]

[2.16] True knowledge of God comes only from the Torah. Without revelation one is left only with primordial nature. Man would live on the level of a beast. The Torah is the sole source of authentic tradition, first for Jews and then for those peoples influenced by Judaism.

> We must seek to explain the great wisdom of the Torah... Even the gentile nations have taken it up and studied it. Do they not have on their own statutes and laws analogous to the statutes and ordinances of the Torah? The explanation – indeed, the first principle everyone should know – is that everything whatever that prophets know and understand is the fruit (*peirot*) of the Torah or the fruit of its fruit. Without it there would be no difference at all between a man and the ass on which he rides. So you see today among those nations that are far from the land of the Torah and prophecy... they do not recognize the Creator but think the world is eternal (*qadmon*). [KR: *Torat ha-Shem Temimah* - I, 142]

The assumption that the world is eternal leads to the belief that nothing changes and that God and man are locked in an immutable pattern. If that were so, neither divine miracles nor human freedom and responsibility would be possible (see Maimonides, *Moreh*, 2.25).

[2.17] Nahmanides recognizes that certain truths can be learned apart from the revelation of the Torah, but he is unwilling to assign real independence to human reason. What is not revealed directly depends on revelation indirectly. All knowledge is ultimately conditioned by sacred history and sacred geography.

Maimonides too emphasizes how the nations far from the Land of Israel seem to be less enlightened than the rest about God and the universe (*Moreh*, 3.51). For him, it is not absolutely necessary, but it is the normal prerequisite to rational theology, (*Igrot ha-Rambam*, ed. Shailat [Jerusalem: Ma'aliyot, 1988] II, 681; *Hilkhot Shemittah ve-Yovel*, 13.13). Reason, however, gives revelation an epistemic ground. For Nahmanides, historical revelation, direct or indirect, is the basis of all authentic theology.

In assigning primacy to the historical/geographical site of Israel's revelation, Nahmanides is clearly the disciple of Halevi (*Kuzari*, 1.95). But he takes a famous text of Maimonides [*Hilkhot Melakhim*, chap. 11, uncensored ed.] as a precedent:

> Do not be confused by the thought that even the nations inherit the Torah. For this is so only with those near the center of the settled world (*ha-yishuv*), such as the Christians and Muslims. For they copied and learned it [T. Sotah 8.6]. When Rome conquered some of the extremities of the earth, they learned the Torah from her and made statutes and laws modelled (*dugma*) after the Torah. But those people who dwell in the extremities of the earth but did not learn Torah and did not see Israel and its way of life (*minhagam*), or who did not hear about them, because of the barrier of geography, are

> complete animals... That is why Maimonides said that all these things [the teachings of Jesus and Muhammad]... are to prepare the way for the Messiah-King. [KR: *Torat ha-Shem Temimah* - I, 143-44]

[2.18] Man's direct relationship with God begins with God, "whose eyes are on the faithful (*ne'emanei*) of the earth" [Gen. 39:8].

> With men of this high level, it is fitting that their souls be bound up in the bond of life, even while they are physically alive... and all their deeds are continually with the Lord... their aim is not to separate from the Lord. [CT: Deut. 11:22 - II, 395]

[2.19] The highest knowledge of God is not to be inferred from ordinary experience of the world, or even from the extraordinary experience of miracles. Without the proper foundation in the soul, even one who witnessed miracles would simply assume that the event was accidental rather than revelatory. Coincidences are just the opposite of the miraculous. They are *less* important than ordinary experiences. Describing Abraham as the paradigm of faith, Nahmanides contrasts his experience of the extraordinary with that of his pagan contemporaries:

> The nations who did not have faith that God performed a miracle (*nes*) for Abraham would not augment their faith in God when they saw his miracle for the king of Sodom... They would believe that all the miracles were accomplished by means of witchcraft or were accidental (*miqreh*). [CT: Gen. 14:10 - I, 85-86]

[2.20] If humans are capable of a direct relationship with God, it is only because God has so predisposed us. Thus, although Nahmanides is sympathetic to Maimonides' opposition to anthropomorphism and like Maimonides upholds God's transcendence of nature, he rejects Maimonides' removal of God from direct, conscious contact with the world and its contingencies:

> Maimonides wrote in the *Moreh Nevukhim* [1.27]... that Onqelos usually made every effort to remove corporeality (*gashmut*) from God in every narrative in the Torah... But if things are as Maimonides says... why does Onqelos nowhere eliminate the attribution to God of speaking, talking and calling... This is Onqelos' practice throughout the Torah [Gen. 21:23]... those who swear do not say "I swear by the word (*ma'amar*) of God"... the hidden meaning of these things (*sodam*) is known to the discerning. [CT: Gen. 46:1 - I, 246-49]

The fact that one can take an oath directly in the name of God indicates the immediacy of the relationship between God and man and hints that the oath (*shevu'ah*) answers an inner divine need (see CT: Num. 30:3 - II, 323 re *Sifre Bemidbar*, ed. Horovitz, no. 153). Thus Nahmanides reasons that Onqelos' removal of anthropomorphism is intended only to remove the ascription of *physical* needs to God. Maimonides erred in assuming that Onqelos intended to remove the ascription of *any* need to God.

[2.21] Knowledge of God, for Nahmanides, is knowledge of God's power and will to accomplish all things. It is anticipation of providence and its works before God's will is actually manifest in a particular situation.

Thus, explaining the verse, "And he had faith in the Lord, and he accounted it to him as righteousness (*tsedaqah*)" [Gen.15:6], Nahmanides does not attribute the righteousness to Abraham as the man of faith but argues that Abraham's faith had the righteousness of God as its object. The verse should be undertsood as saying: "And Abram had faith in the Lord's righteousness and credited the Lord with it." Faith does not make its bearer righteous. Faith is human certitude that God is righteous, that God has both the power and the will to keep his promises. 'Righteousness' here is understood as charity:

> The sound interpretation seems to me to be that when it says "he had faith in the Lord" he believed that God, in his charity, would give him children – not because of the righteousness of Abraham... or his own sin could impede it. [CT: Gen. 15:6 - I, 90]

The familiar interpretation of the verse is that Abraham's faith counts as his righteousness. See, e.g., LXX *ad loc.*; 1 Macc. 2:52; *Tanhuma,* printed ed.: Be-shalah, 10; Bahya ibn Pakudah, *Hovot ha-Levavot*: Sha'ar ha-Bitahon, chap. 4. Paul (Romans 4:20-22) uses such a reading to argue for the primacy of faith over the Torah's specific commandments. As an experienced respondent to Christian anti-Jewish polemics, Nahmanides' clearly had such readings in mind. The fideistic interpretation lent itself too readily to Paul's case.

Nahmanides' line of interpretation is followed by many later kabbalists (*Zohar*: Naso, 3:148a; Isaiah Halevi Horowitz, *Shnei Luhot ha-Berit (Shalah)*, 3, Torah she-bi-Khtav: Lekh Lekha, end). More concerned with divine than with human reality, the kabbalists value an interpretation that has the verse address God's attributes rather than Abraham's.

[2.22] God's power and will to keep his promises for the ultimate good of his human creation is rooted in God's creativity, which is unlimited by any antecedent or coequal factors. This divine creativity is what faith ultimately apprehends:

> According to the view of men of faith... the world is something created *ex nihilo* by the absolute will of God. [CT: Gen. 2:17 - I, 38]

This, for Nahmanides, is "the root (*shoresh*) of faith" [CT: Gen 1:1 - I, 9].

[2.23] Just as God's charity is the source of his providence over humankind, so human faith is the source of the actions that enable us to live in intimacy with God. Here again Abraham is the paradigm. Nahmanides comments on the Torah's reiteration of God's covenant with Abraham to his son Isaac:

> One could say that "my charge" [Gen. 26:5] refers to faith in God. For Abraham had faith in the unique God and kept his charge in his heart. It was by this means that he argued against idolatry and called upon the name of the Lord to turn many to his service. [CT: Gen. 26:5 -I, 151]

[2.24] Because faith is the motive of action, absence of faith is more serious than absence of any specific action (see B. Baba Kama 16b, Tos., s.v. *ve-hu* re M. Sanhedrin 10.1). Glossing the verse "cursed be he who does not uphold (*yaqim*) the words of this Torah to do them," Nahmanides writes:

> In my view, the commitment called for here (*ha-qabbalah ha-zo't*) is that one should acknowledge the commandments in his heart and regard them as true. He should have faith that one who performs them will be well requited... And if he denies any one of them or declares any one of them permanently abrogated (*betelah le-'olam*) – such a person is accursed. [CT: Deut. 27:26 - II, 472]

Here Nahmanides rejects both legalism, the view that the commandments are simply to be performed, that inner conviction is irrelevant, and the Pauline view that faith takes the place of the commandments (Galatians 3:10 quoting LXX on Deut. 27:26 - "all [*pasin*] the words of this Law").

[2.25] For Nahmanides, faith is the certitude not only in what God has done, but also in what God still does. Thus faith is the true foundation of all action; for faith alone can determine the proper intention of action.

> The first commandment is the positive commandment obliging a person to search, inquire and seek to know God's divinity. We find this to be a positive commandment: "You shall know today and take it to heart [that the Lord is God in the heavens above and the earth below, there is none else]" (Deut. 4:39). There is a hint in the words, "I am the Lord your

> God" (Exod. 20:2) that knowledge of this is the foundation and root (*ha-yesod ve-ha-shoresh*) of all. It was apropos of this that our Rabbis, of blessed memory, said that whenever one has knowledge (*de'ah*), it is as if the Temple had been rebuilt in his days [B. Berakhot 36a]. The thrust of this statement is that one who knows how to affirm the unity of God's unique Name (*le-yahed shem ha-meyuhad*) has, as it were, built the structure (*paltrin*) of what is above and what is below... After such knowledge the work of divine service (*mel'ekhet 'avodah*) is now within him. [KR: *Explanation of the 613 Commandments Proceeding from the Decalogue* - II, 521]

What Nahmanides means by this last sentence is that the person who has true knowledge of God (presumably learned from Kabbalah) will be able to perform the commandments according to their true intentions, aware of how God is both their source and their ultimate end.

[2.26] Maimonides had counted belief in God as the first of the 248 positive commandments of the Written Torah. He differed here with the influential ninth century work, *Halakhot Gedolot*, which did not count the first item in the Decalogue in its enumeration of the 613 traditional commandments. Nahmanides agrees with the author of *Halakhot Gedolot*, not just because of his usual preference for an earlier authority, but for a theological reason. He takes it that the presupposition necessary to the authority of all the commandments cannot itself be among them. For Maimonides, God's existence was a matter of rational demonstration. In such a context, one can perhaps understand the commandment to believe in God as a prescription demanding that we pursue the theological knowledge represented by such a proof. But Nahmanides avows that the existence of God is to be experienced through God's mighty deeds, which are his self-revelation to us:

> Evidently it was the view of the author of *Halakhot Gedolot* that the 613 commandments include only his decrees upon us, exalted be he, to do or refrain from some act. But faith (*emunah*) in his exalted existence, which he made known to us by signs and manifestations (*u-moftim*) and the revelation of his Presence (*giluy Shekhinah*) before our very eyes, is the root and the source (*ha-'iqqar ve-ha-shoresh*) from which the commandments spring... Wherever you may be, it is a commandment that it be said: "Know and believe that I the Lord took you out of the land of Egypt; now do my commandments." Even so, this is not to be included in the actual count of the commandments. For it is the root, and they are the offshoots. [*Notes on Maimonides' Sefer ha-Mitzvot*, pos. no. 1, p. 152]

The Talmudic basis of the doctrine of 613 commandments of the Written Torah is in B. Makkot 23a-24a. Careful examination of the text there seems to support Maimonides' position. For "I am the Lord your God" is seen as the first of the 613 commandments. The general theological principles of Judaism, as distinct from the specific commandments, are discussed separately. Yet Maimonides was frequently criticized for what was seen as his confusion of law and theology in regard to this passage. See Hasdai ibn Crescas, *Or ha-Shem*, intro.; Joseph Albo, *Sefer ha-'Iqqarim*, 1.14; and my *Law and Theology in Judaism*, **1**, ch. 15.

[2.27] To know and have faith in God is a commandment for Nahmanides. But the relevant knowledge comes directly from the experience of the Exodus and needs no separate precept. It is presupposed by the 613 precepts of the Written Torah; for one must acknowledge God to perform any of the commandments with the proper intention (*kavvanah*):

> This sentence ["I am the Lord your God] is a positive commandment... instructing and commanding them to know and have faith that the Lord exists and is their God, the primordial Being from whom all came to be, by his will and power. He is their God, whom they must serve... and the obligation is, in the words of the Rabbis, "acceptance of the sovereignty of God (*qabbalat malkhut Shamayim*)." [CT: Exod. 20:2 - I, 388]

The source in the Mishnah (Berakhot 2.2) presents acceptance of God's sovereignty as leading directly to acceptance of the comamndments. See also *Mekhilta*: Yitro, ed. Horovitz-Rabin, 219; *Midrash Leqah Tov*: Aharei Mot, ed. S. Buber, 50b.

[2.28] The commandment to accept the Lord God, who took Israel out of Egypt, then becomes the archetype of all the subsequent commandments:

> When it says, "I took you out," this is to remind them that they already knew, as was manifest to them at the Exodus from Egypt, that there is a God who made the world *de novo*, who knows particulars and exercises providence over them. [KR: *Torat ha-Shem Temimah* - I, 152]

[2.29] For Nahmanides faith manifests itself through action. Acts of faith are tests of human willingness to obey God despite the ordinary expectations of the world. Human potential for faith is actualized in the deeds that make faith efficacious. In Jewish tradition, Abraham's acceptance of God's command to sacrifice his son Isaac has always been the paradigm of obedience to God's will:

> A trial (*nissayon*) is so called because of the one who is tried, but the One who tries him, exalted be he, commands it in order to bring the matter from potentiality to actuality, so that the one tried may receive the reward deserved for action, not just for having a good heart... and so, with all the trials in the Torah. They are for the good of the one who is tried. [CT: Gen. 22:1 - I, 125-26]

[2.30] In an earlier discussion of the trial of Abraham, Nahmanides raises the perplexing question how divine foreknowledge and human free choice can be reconciled:

> Why did he try (*menasseh*) him when it is clearly known to Him, exalted be he, whether or not a particular saint will accept the task and the challenge? Because, be that as it may, a person's reward is not for his faith. That would be nothing like the reward for an actual deed. So God lend assistance by bringing one's good character to action. Why, then, is it called a "trial" (*nissayon*)? Is it not the case that "everything is known to Him" (M. Avot 3.15)? ...Even so [as the same text continues], "one has free choice (*reshut*)" to do it if he wants; and if one does not want to do it, he will not do it. Thus... it is called the trial of the one performing the act, but not the trial of the One who commands it, exalted be his name. [KR: *Torat ha-'Adam*: Sha'ar ha-Gemul - II, 272]

The fourteenth century Spanish Jewish theologian, Hasdai ibn Crescas developed this notion more philosophically. He argued that human freedom of choice is based on our ignorance of future events. God the Creator knows everything: past, present and future. But even if everything is preordained by God, human beings cannot know exactly what is preordained. So freedom of choice is a subjective requirement. We must act *as if* everything were not preordained (see *Or ha-Shem*, 2.5.3-5). Some later kabbalists, building on the doctrine of *tsimtsum* (divine self-contraction) were bolder (and more cogent) on this question than either Nahmanides or Crescas, arguing that God might have limited his own knowledge of future events for the sake of human freedom. See the 18th century Italian kabbalist Hayyim ibn Attar, *Commentary on the Torah*: Gen. 6:5; cf. my "The Doctrine of the Self-Contraction of God in Kabbalistic Theology," in L. E. Goodman, ed. *Neoplatonism and Jewish Thought*, 292-93.

[2.31] God's miraculous disruptions of the familiar order of the world serve not to establish faith but to make the world too uncertain for us to seek ultimate certitude in it.

> Moses believed that God spoke with him. But perhaps, even though he made known to him the great Name through which all things came into being, he wanted to show him that through it signs and manifestations would be worked, changing the normal course of events (*ha-toldot*). This was to confirm it in the heart of Moses, that he might know in truth that by God's hand new things would be done in the world. [CT: Exod. 4:3 - I, 295]

Nahmanides distinguishes here between God as perceived through the natural order (*Elohim*) and God as he presents himself to Israel in revelation. The tetragrammaton designates God's self-presentation. See CT: Exod. 8:15 (I, 312-13) following Ibn Ezra *ad loc.*

[2.32] God's miraculous incursions into nature, by shaking our confidence in nature redirect our trust to what transcends nature. We have already seen that without the proper predisposition faith will not arise even from the experience of miracles. Yet that experience strengthens the predisposition. Since miracles are not part of our experience at present, the commandments of the Torah enable believers to relive them and thus apprehend their meaning. Such participation is far more than cognitive:

> These are the commandments [*tefillin*, circumcision, the Sabbath] that acknowledge the uniqueness (*ha-yihud*) of God and serve to remind us of all the commandments and their several rewards and punishments. The whole root (*shoresh*) is in faith... Indeed, from the time that idolatry began in the world, from the days of Enosh, views about faith have grown confused... So the great signs and manifestations are reliable witnesses of the Creator and the entire Torah. Thus God did not perform signs and manifestations in every generation, to be seen by every wicked person and nonbeliever. Rather, he commanded us to make a perpetual reminder and sign of what our eyes saw. [CT: Exod. 13:16 - I, 145-46]

[2.33] Direct knowledge of God was lost through sin. The spread of human knowledge of God's miracles can restore that lost knowledge:

> But the Lord created man among the lower creatures so that he might recognize his Creator and acknowledge his Name. And he placed the power in his hands to do evil or to do good. But when they sinned willingly and all of them denied him, only this people was left for his Name, and he made it known that he is God through them, by signs and manisfestations. [CT: Deut. 32:26 - II, 489]

[2.34] All of the commandments refer to the Exodus from Egypt as *the* demonstration (*mofet*) of God's transcendence of nature and absolute freedom. Discussing God's power and providence, Nahmanides writes:

> For the Exodus from Egypt teaches all of these points perfectly... Indeed, even a "light" commandment teaches all of the fundaments of faith and perfection. Thus it says, "Be as careful with a light commandment (*mitsvah qalah*) as with a weighty one (*mitsvah hamurah*), for you do not know the reward of the commandments" [M. Avot 2.1]. For all of them are reminders of the miracle and the favor he performed for our ancestors and for us. And in all of them there is evidence (*re'ayah*) in support of faith. That is why we are accustomed to recall the the Exodus from Egypt in all our commandments. [KR: *Torat ha-Shem Temimah* - I, 151]

Nahmanides' point is best understood in the light of the rabbinic discussions of the difference between "light" and "heavy" commandments. In one tannaitic opinion, heavy commandments are those for whose violation divinely administered excision (*karet*) or humanly administered execution is mandated. All other comandments are deemed light (M. Yoma 8.8; T. Kippurim 4.5 and Saul Lieberman, *Tosefta Kifshuta*: Moed [JTS, 1962], 823). In a second tannaitic opinion, light commandments are those involving lesser expense; heavy ones are those involving greater expense (M. Hullin 12.5). In an amoraic opinion, light commandments are those one can rarely perform; heavy are those one can perform regularly (Y. Kiddushin 1.10/61d re M. Peah 1.1; see David Weiss Halivni, *Meqorot u-Mesorot*: Mo'ed, 662). Honoring one's parents would thus an example of the former; sending away the mother bird before taking her young from the nest (*shiluah ha-qan* - Deut. 22:6-7), of the latter (see B. Kiddushin 39b; Hullin 142a; Y. Peah 1.1 / 15d; Y. Kiddushin 1.7 / 61b).

The fourteenth century Provencal commentator, Menahem Meiri adds a more theological rationale for the distinction. Explaining the Talmudic requirement that candidates for conversion to Judaism to be instructed in "some of the light commandments and some of the heavy commandments" (B. Yevamot 47a), he understands a distinction between more specific (light mitsvot) and more general duties (heavy mitsvot). The specific commandments are more distinctively Jewish, so they are more likely to discourage a gentile from conversion, since the duties expected in gentile religions are more general (*Bet ha-Behirah*: Yevamot, ed. S. Dickman [Jerusalem: Makhon ha-Talmud ha-Yisraeli ha-Shalem, 1968], 189; cf. Y. Berakhot 1.5 / 3c; Maimonides, *Commentary on the Mishnah*: Tamid 5.1). A certain measure of discouragement against conversion to Judaism is the norm that affords the background of Meiri's interpretation.

It is the sense of the distinction between light and heavy developed by Meiri that seems closest to Nahmanides here. For him, seemingly trivial specific commandments assume a cosmic significance when understood as active symbols of and participations in God's manifestations in the history of Israel. Thus in commenting on Exodus 13:16 (CT: I, 346), again quoting from M. Avot 2.1, Nahmanides writes: "For one can purchase a *mezuzah* for just one zuz and affix it to his doorpost with proper intention of its significance and thereby affirm the creation of the world, the omniscience and providence of the Creator, and express faith in prophecy and in all the foundations (*pinot*) of the Torah." In ontological terms, there are no "light" commandments (see Maimonides, *Commentary on the Mishnah*: Avot 2.1 re B. Sukkah 25a).

Chapter 3

Tradition

[3.1] Nahmanides was keenly aware that immediate knowledge of God is an exalted, prophetic state, beyond the capacity of ordinary people. Some mediation is needed between the direct knowledge of God and ordinary human knowledge. But such mediation cannot come through knowledge of the physical world. For nature has no consciousness of God. Tradition takes on the critical role of conveying such knowledge. Its credibility comes from our faith in the truthfulness of our parents. The most basic factor in childhood identity, "Whose child am I?", can be a matter of certitude only when the child has faith in the parental intentions. Parents, then, are not only the biological link between the child and creation, but also the noetic link with it. They establish the trust that will enable religious faith to emerge. The veracity of Jewish tradition rests on the trustworthiness of the ancestors. The source of the tradition is divine truth, and in Nahmanides' view only the moral fault of human deceit, not the intellectual fault of human error, could make this tradition untrue. But deceit by our forebears is unthinkable. The tradition we receive from them cannot be doubted. Of the Sinai experience, Nahmanides writes:

> The value (*ha-to'elet*) of this commandment is immense. For if the words of the Torah came to us only from the mouth of Moses... then if a prophet or a dreamer arose in our midst and commanded us to act contrary to the Torah... doubt would enter the hearts of men. But since the Torah comes from the mouth of God (*mi-pi ha-Gevurah*) to our ears, and we saw with our own eyes that there was no intermediary (*emtsa'i*), we can refute all who dispute it and belie all who doubt it... For when we tell it to our children, they know that this was true. Without a doubt, it is as if (*ke'ilu*) all the generations saw it for them-

> selves. For we would not bequeath them something vain (*hevel*) and useless. [CT: Deut. 4:9 - II, 362]

[3.2] Nahmanides reads the Torah's presentation of genealogies as showing that tradition was transmitted from eyewitnesses to their descendents without interruption, preserving the reliability the account:

> It is clear why these families and their dwelling places [are mentioned] and why it is that they were dispersed throughout the world: to validate (*l'ammet*) the account of creation. If one finds it hard to understand how near creation was... the Torah removes this doubt by recalling the genealogy of the families, their names, and the reason for their dispersion and change of languages... For there were only three generations from Adam to the Flood, and each had received the tradition from its father. [KR: *Torat ha-Shem Temimah* - I, 170]

[3.3] In support of the veracity of Scriptural tradition, Nahmanides writes:

> The Torah enlightens the eyes even in its stories and narratives. For all of them are of great wisdom and foundational to our faith. For you know from the overt sense of the Scriptural verses that Amram, the father of Moses, saw Levi, who saw Jacob, who learned Torah from Shem the son of Noah... Moses... [in effect] publicly stated, "my father told me this"... Moreover, Shem the son of Noah saw Adam... If this were false, everyone would have known about it and it would have been refuted by many elders and sages of the people who knew history (*divrei ha-yamim*). For all of us know of these public events from the mouth of our elders. [KR: *Torat ha-Shem Temimah* - I, 144]

[3.4] Tradition is clearly a necessity for those whose faith is still developing. This process of development is not simply an individual project; it involves the transmission of authentic tradition from one generation to the next. In moving forward in the knowledge of God, the one "on the way" reaches back across the generations for guidance. Nahmanides illustrates:

> For Noah saw his father, who saw the first man... and men in every generation know (*yod'im*) from their fathers. [CT: Gen. 10:5 - I, 65]

[3.5] Our connection, by authentic tradition, with the primal events of sacred history rests on what might be called patriarchal emanation: A human father's authority has its source and limit in God's primordial fatherhood:

> A father is to his descendents like a creator, a partner in the act of formation. For the Lord is our first father, and our human progenitor (*ve-ha-moleed*) is our ultimate father. [CT: Exod. 20:12 - I, 403]

[3.6] Although parents are "second creators," honoring them is not an end in itself like the recognition of God, which is foundational:

> Now what the human person is commanded regarding faith in God is completed. It begins with the father. For as I command you to honor the first Creator, so I command you to give honor to the second, who gave you being, your father and mother. Thus it says, "in order that your days may be long [on the land which the Lord your God gives you]" (Exod. 20:12). For it is a commandment concerning earthly beings (*tahtonim*) and requires external reward. But the commandment regarding faith in the Creator does not need a reason (*ta'am*) to establish its validity. [KR: *Torat ha-Shem Temimah* - I, 152]

[3.7] Nahmanides' emphasis on the inextricable link between tradition and revelation is clearly visible in his dispute with Maimonides over the status of rabbinic legal exegesis (*derash*) of the Written Torah. The Rabbis differentiated two types of legal exegesis. When they called an interpretation "a matter of Torah" (*dvar Torah*), they meant that the interpretation is the prescriptive *denotation* of Scripture (e.g., B. Baba Metsia 47b). When they called an interpretation *asmakhta*, they meant that the interpretation is only the prescriptive *connotation* of the text (e.g., B. Pesahim 81b). Here a norm formulated by the Rabbis is linked to an approriate verse in Scripture.

Most often the Rabbis did not label their exegesis (reading out of a text) or their eisegesis (reading into a text) by either term. All undesignated interpretations for Maimonides have the lesser status of connotative interpretations. In general he plays down tradition in favor of independent reason in Halakhah (see, esp., *Hilkhot Mamrim*, 1.1 ff.; and my "Maimonides and the Science of the Law", *Jewish Law Association Studies* [1990] IV, 99 ff.). But for Nahmanides tradition is our only connection with history, and it is in history rather than nature that God is most manifest. Nahmanides' conception of the continuity of tradition and Scripture leads him to the striking affirmation that ultimately all the commandments the Rabbis derived from Scripture by exegesis are Biblical:

> If these [commandments the Rabbis learned through the principles of legal exegesis] branch out from these [Scriptural] roots, they are still part of them... Although not counted as separate commandments, it is nevertheless proper to call them "words of Torah," even if they are not numbered among the 613

> commandments... Thus we hold contrary to what Maimonides says: anything derived via the thirteen principles of legal exegesis has Scriptural status (*mi-d'oraitia*) unless we hear the rabbis explicitly designate it as *asmakhta*. [*Notes on Maimonides' Sefer ha-Mitzvot*, intro., sec. 2, pp. 32, 34]

Most subsequent Talmudists favored the traditionalist approach of Nahmanides over the rationalist approach of Maimonides here (see, e.g., Yom Tov ben Abraham Ishbili, *Hiddushei ha-Ritba*: Rosh Hashanah 16a). In glossing Talmudic texts where the line between Torah law and rabbinic law was obscure, some later Talmudists (*aharonim*) in fact sometimes fell back on the position of Nahmanides, that ultimately there is no difference (e.g., Samuel Strashun, *Hagahot ve-Hiddushei ha-Rashash*: Gittin 49b).

[3.8] Nahmanides' valuation of the authority of precedent, simply on the grounds of its antiquity can be seen in his position on a fundamental medieval dispute about the requisites for repealing rabbinic legislation. The Talmud (B. 'Avodah Zarah 36a) ruled that a rabbinic law may be repealed by later authorities if it was not accepted by the majority of Israel. Rashi (s.v. *lo pashat*) takes this as referring to the time of the promulgation of the law. A related passage ('Avodah Zarah 35a) states that the reason for no rabbinic law should be revealed for a year, providing time to ascertain whether the proposed law had gained popular acceptance. Presumably, without such acceptance a reason would be superfluous. But once a rabbinic law had gained acceptance, popular rejection would not suffice for its repeal.

For Maimonides, any disuse, even long after the first promulgation of a rabbinic law, suffices for its formal repeal by a later court (*Hilkhot Mamrim*, 2.7; see Joseph Karo, *Kesef Mishneh ad loc.*). Nahmanides' respect for the authority of tradition leads to his concurrence with Rashi:

> You should know that the decree of the disciples of Shammai and Hillel as to not eating bread baked by gentiles was one that most of the community were unable to keep... I say that if the sages and leading authorities of Israel (*gedoleihem*) were to agree in permitting bread baked by gentiles, it would be permitted, even if their stature were less than that of the disciples of Shammai and Hillel in both wisdom and numbers [of disciples]... With any rabbinic decree (*gezerah*) which the majority of the community are understood to be able to obey, repeal requires a subsequent court greater than the original one in both in wisdom and numbers [M. 'Eduyot 1.5]. But only if it did not actually become the common practice of Israel. If the decree has become common practice (*pashtah*), no subsequent court may repeal it. [*Hiddushei ha-Ramban ha-Shalem*: 'Avodah Zarah 35b, pp. 98-99]

[3.9] Nahmanides does not tire of insisting that "the all-encompassing principle is that the tradition (*ha-qabbalah*) is always true" [CT: Exod. 21:22/ 1:425]. It is for this reason that the narrative portions of the Torah carry normative import and are more than mere backgrounds to the explicitly prescriptive portions:

> The Torah includes the stories (*sippurim*) from the beginning of Genesis on. It instructs (*moreh*) men progressing in the matter of faith. [CT: Introduction - I, 1]

[3.10] Following the teaching of the Midrash [*Shemot Rabbah* 3.11; 5.1], Nahmanides argues that the reason the people of Israel first listened to Moses when he returned to Egypt from Midian was that they had an ancestral tradition "that Joseph handed down (*masrah*) to Levi, saying that Jacob revealed his mystical message (*galah sodo*) to Joseph in love" [CT: Exod. 3:18 - I, 294]. The message was that the first who would come and use the words of Joseph, "God will surely be mindful (*paqod yifqod*) of you" (Gen. 50:26), was to be accepted as their redeemer sent by God. And Moses was indeed the one who said to them, "the Lord, God of your fathers, appeared to me... saying, 'I am surely mindful (*paqod paqadti*) of you, of what is being done to you in Egypt'" (Exod. 3:16).

[3.11] The primacy Nahmanides assigns tradition seems to be at odds with the well known Talmudic statement that "from the day the Temple was destroyed prophecy was taken from the prophets but not from the sages" [B. Baba Batra 12a]. This dictum is often taken to mean that reason now functions as an independent force in the shaping of Judaism. But Nahmanides' sees in the passage a distinction between higher and lower inspiration:

> What the passage means is this: Even though the prophecy of the prophets has been removed, that is, revelations and visions, the prophecy of the sages, that is, the method of wisdom, has not been taken away. For they know the truth through the holy spirit within their inmost being (*be-qirbam*). According to the needs of the moment God makes his presence dwell on the pious, even if they are not sages. [*Hidushei ha-Ramban*: B. Baba Batra 12a, p. 105]

[3.12] In a striking interpretation of an oft cited Talmudic passage concerning R. Eliezer ben Hyrkanus, Nahmanides demonstrates just how far he carries his traditionalism. The venerable sage was placed under a ban for refusing to accept the ruling of his colleagues in a matter of Halakhah. Despite his invocation of supernatural phenomena in support of his stance, they refused to accept it. R. Eliezer's obstinancy is usually ascribed to a refusal to accept anything but explicit tradition as the basis of a norm (see

B. Sukkah 28a). But Nahmanides reads the passage as showing that the majority had tradition on their side: Tradition took precedence over the arguments and even the supernatural phenomena invoked by R. Eliezer:

> Actually, R. Eliezer was liable only to be placed under a temporary ban (*niddui*), which is used when a rabbi's honor is at issue [here, the honor of his colleague, R. Joshua, which he seemed to make light of in his polemical remarks], as with Aqabiah ben Mehallalel [see M. 'Eduyot 5.6-7]. Some say that because he did not want to relent and said... "a voice from heaven will vindicate my opinion," his position appeared to be heresy (*ke'afqaruta*); he was overly prolonging the dispute, so they placed him under an indefinite ban (*berkuhu*). For what they held was based on a specific tradition (*mi-pi ha-shemu'ah*). But what he said was his personal opinion (*kakh hu b'einei*). That is why they did not accept any of his proofs. Had he so ruled in the days of the Temple, he would have been declared an elder in contempt of the Sanhedrin (*zaqen mamre*). Accordingly, they were strict with him, placing him under an indefinite ban. [*Hiddushei ha-Ramban*: B. Baba Metzia 59b, p. 53]

Strikingly, Baba Metsia does not state that R. Eliezer presented his opinion as his own. But Nahmanides applies a passage from another context, B. Sanhedrin 88a, which holds that a *zaqen mamre* was to be executed if he said "such appears to me" but his colleagues in the Sanhedrin said, "it is a tradition (*mi-pi ha-shemu'ah*)." (I thank David Weiss Halivni for clarifying this point to me.)

[3.13] Nahmanides rejects Aristotle as a guide to true knowledge of God because he "rejected all truth but what he could experience through his senses (*ha-murgash lo*)... For whatever he did not grasp with his own intelligence was assumed to be untrue" (CT: Lev. 16:8 - II, 91). It was bad enough that Aristotle lacked revelation, but far worse for Jews, who had received the Torah, to attempt to constitute religious knowledge without it. It is doubtful that Nahmanides ever read Aristotle, but his objection is not so much against the philosopher himself as it is against those Jewish theologians, especially Maimonides, who sought to ground Jewish thinking on such an inadequate foundation as Aristotelian philosophy.

[3.14] Aristotle's thought, Nahmanides argues, rests on too narrow a base. Had he not lacked revelation and an older tradition (cf. Plato, *Timaeus* 22B), he would not have inferred the impossibility of any real innovation in the world:

> He denies a number of things that many have seen. We ourselves witnessed their truth, and they are known (*ve-nitparsemu*) throughout the world... Because of their [the earliest generations of human beings] propinquity to the creation of the world and to the Flood, there was no one who denied the creation of the world *de novo* or rebelled against God himself... But when the Greeks arose, a new people who did not inherit wisdom, as Halevi explains in the *Kuzari* [1.65], this well-known man [Aristotle] arose, who believed only in the sensory characteristics of nature (*pe'ulah raq le-tiv'im*). Yet it is well and widely known (*u-mefursam*) that this is incorrect. [KR: *Torat ha-Shem Temimah* - I, 147]

[3.15] Nahmanides holds that revelation provides knowledge to which philosophers aspire but never achieve by their independent efforts, a point made earlier by Halevi (*Kuzari*, 1.4; 4.13; 5.14):

> None of the philosophers knows about the created order (*ba-yetsirah*) what the least in Israel does know. For clearly the value (*to'elet*) of the other sciences is only as a ladder to that wisdom which is called "knowledge of the Creator." [KR: *Torat ha-Shem Temimah* - I, 155]

[3.16] Nahmanides underscores the difference between man-made thought and wisdom from God in contrasting Elihu with the other friends of Job:

> One sees that once he heard the words of Elihu, Job did not answer him at all. This indeed shows us that his answer was new, not like that of the other friends... One sees that the arguments of the friends were opinions that grew out of their own thoughts... We do not find that any of them called their arguments wisdom (*hokhmah*)... but with Elihu, all of his words are called wisdom, for example: "Be silent and I will relate to you marvelous wisdom" (Job 33:33)... This is an indication that his argument was unique and that it was revealed wisdom, coming from the men of the Torah and prophets. [KR: *Commentary on Job* 32:2 - I, 96-97]

[3.17] Because recognition of God presupposes revelation and tradition, Nahmanides credits the ancient view that Job was an Edomite, descended from Abraham and Isaac through Esau. That is why he could recognize God and observe the rational commandments:

> Thus it is probable that this man was of the seed of Abraham, an Edomite. He acknowledged his Creator and served him by way of the rational commandments (*ha-mitsvot ha-sikhliyot*)... Scripture mentions that these men, Job and his friends, were of the seed of the man [Abraham] who was the founder of faith. They still preserved his way, as it is written, "for I know him that he will command his children and his household after him, etc." (Gen. 18:19). [KR: *Commentary on Job* 1:1 - I, 27]

Nahmanides here follows a rabbinic opinion that Job was a gentile (B. Baba Batra 15a-b; Bereshit Rabbah 57.4, ed. Theodor-Albeck, 614, 617). But many rabbinic sources assume that he was a Jew (see Louis Ginzberg, *Legends of the Jews*, **5**.381-82, n. 3).

[3.18] To Aristotelian Jewish theologians history seemed to pertain to the realm of the ephemeral and thus to lack real intelligibility. But for Nahmanides, as for Halevi, history held in memory by the people of Israel, reveals God as "the Overseer (*ha-manhig*) of time by his power" (CT: Gen. 21:33 - I, 1125). Yet Nahmanides' historical vision is not focused on development. Like the ancients, he regarded change as insignificant. Rather, history for him was the manifestation of unique events, to be retold and relived in ritual. These events become the archetypes of all subsequent communal experiences of the presence of God. As he puts it, "the entire Torah is the history (*toldot*) of man" (CT: Gen. 5:1 - I, 47).

Maimonides finds historical development even within the Torah, but Nahmanides will have none of this. For him, the Torah is all of a piece. It is, most immediately, the divine perspective on the human condition. But ultimately, it is the script of an inner divine drama in which certain blessed Jews are granted supporting roles. In proposing this view, Nahmanides laid the foundation for the kabbalistic understanding of the Torah, which finds the true meaning of the commandments in their portent as symbolic expressions of the divine life:

> Maimonides in the *Guide of the Perplexed* [3.46] said that the reason for the sacrifices is that... the Israelites had to be cured of corrupt beliefs, which are a disease of the soul... but these are hollow words (*divrei hava'i*)... It is sounder to accept the explanation that because the deeds of human beings comprise thought, word and act, so did the Lord command that when one sins and brings a sacrifice, he presses his hands on it – corresponding to the deed – confesses with his mouth – corresponding to speech – and burns the intestines and kidneys, the instruments of thought and lust... This interpretation appeals to the imagination, like *aggadah*. But, according to the

> way of deeper truth (*derekh ha-'emet*), there is a hidden mystery (*sod ne'elam*) about the sacrifices. [CT: Lev. 1:9 - II, 11-12]

Nahmanides prefers an aggadic, psychological interpretation of the sacrifices to the historicist interpretation of Maimonides (see, also, CT: Lev. 4:2 - II, 22). He took an eclectic position toward Aggadah (see KR: *Disputation*, sec. 39, I,308), but he clearly regards it as part of the authentic tradition. Rationalist Jewish theology for him was not. Ultimately, the closer Aggadah came to the truth of Kabbalah, the more authentic it seemed to Nahmanides. Indeed he used Kabbalah as a criterion to recast many *aggadot*; see E. R. Wolfson, "By Way of Truth."

[3.19] Nahmanides frequently insists on the compatibility of Aggadah with the higher truth of Kabbalah. In one place he writes, "these are words of Aggadah and they are also words of higher truth' (CT: Exod. 1:1 - I, 280). Although Aggadah is on a lower plane than Kabbalah, it is sometimes given preference to the ostensible meaning (*peshat*) of a verse:

> We should leave the Scriptural verse in its literal meaning (*ke-mashma'uto*) and pursue the midrashic interpretation... This is what seems the deeper meaning of the passage, so the words of the sages might endure. That is what is beautiful and acceptable. [CT: Lev. 14:46 - II, 84]

Chapter 4

Miracles

[4.1] For Nahmanides the act of faith (*emunah*) is the human anticipation of providence. Without such faith, one would not recognize providential power when it is exercised. Providence manifests itself in what Nahmanides calls "secret miracles" (*nissim nistarim*):

> 'God Almighty' (*El Shaddai*)... this name expresses the attribute of power (*ha-Gevurah*) that governs the world here below... The reason it is mentioned now [at God's covenantal promise to Abraham] is that it is through this name that secret miracles are performed for the righteous... like all the miracles performed for Abraham and the other patriarchs, and like... the blessings and curses [that attend Israel's obedience or disobedience to the commandments], all of which are miracles. For it is not by nature that rain should fall in due season because of our service of God... So with all the designated occurrences (*ha-ye'udim*) in the Torah... the influence of the heavenly constellations (*ha-mazalot*) is overcome. Yet these miracles do not depart from the accustomed course of the world (*mi--minhago shel 'olam*), as did the miracles performed by Moses. [CT: Gen. 17:1 - I, 98]

There is no real difference in kabbalistic theology between revelation and creation, so the words of the Torah are all efficacious. All are permutations of the divine names (see Gershom Scholem, *On the Kabbalah and its Symbolism*, trans R. Manheim [New York: Schocken, 1969], 36 ff.). This is clearest when an explicit name is used, as is the case here. Nahmanides stresses the power of God's name to direct the course of nature favorably for the righteous.

[4.2] The secret miracles are hidden in that their ostensible causality is ordinary. It is natural that Judah should be attracted to Tamar. But the outcome of his attraction was fulfillment of God's plan. As in this case, secret miracles require a subsequent revelation to be appreciated. Public miracles (*nissim mefursamim*), by contrast, are evident immediately, since their overt causality is extraordinary.

> The Rabbis say explicitly that R. Huna said in the name of R. Idi, 'One should not say that Tamar fornicated or that Judah desired to fornicate, but that these things were from Me [God]. That is to say (*kelomar*), this was one of the secret miracles constantly found in the Torah, as we have explained. For it was from the blessed Creator that the divine will and determinative decree (*gezerat ratson*) reached the powers proximate to the situation, the angel appointed over this matter [sexual attraction]. There was an emanation from God to the heavenly powers that act on earthly things both in general and in particular. [KR: *Commentary on Job*, intro. - I, 26]

The rabbinic source cited here is not found in any printed text. For a possible manuscript source, see M. M. Kasher, *Torah Shlemah* (New York: n.p., 1948) **6**.1476, n. 114.

[4.3] What public and private miracles have in common to warrant each being called a miracle (*nes*) is that both are understood to be direct expressions of God's will. All other events belong to the natural order, epitomized by the regular movement of the constellations. Secret miracles do not obviously contradict this order. The same event can be interpreted by a nonbeliever as natural and by a believer as miraculous. The essential difference that makes for a miracle is a mere accident for the nonbeliever. Thus what is most important to the believer is least important to the nonbeliever. But public miracles do run counter to the natural order. They shatter normal expectations. Where there is a predisposition for faith, such stunning experiences can remove the impediment to its growth.

Nahmanides speaks of "the miraculous which is evident (*galui*) and public and contrary to nature" (CT: Gen. 46:15 - I, 254). With secret miracles, nothing unfamiliar is seen. What is unusual is the favorable position in the physical world of the person blessed with such a miracle. One can explain naturalistically how and when rain falls. But why it will rain on a particular spot to benefit particular people is not explicable by natural law. Only prior faith in God's power apprehends such a miracle. For God's power alone made the event occur just when and as it did. The combination of outward normality with inward uniqueness was known even to the patriarchs:

> For he appeared to the patriarchs by this name [*El Shaddai*], which means that he subdued the heavenly constellations to perform great miracles through them, miracles that did not void the normal course of the world... But the rewards and punishments of the Torah are all secret miracles, which appear to those who see them as belonging to the normal course of the world, although the truth is that they are punishments and rewards for human beings. [CT: Exod. 6:2 - II, 303]

In Aristotelian physics every species has its own nature or essence, an indelible "form," by which members of the species behave as they must. This behavior expresses each being's inclination toward its own natural end (*inclinatio naturalis*). Once one understands the proper nature of any being, one can predict how it will behave. Gross deviations are impossible. Only nonessential, "accidental" deviations are admitted. These are ascribed to chance factors (Aristotle, *Physics*, 193b 22 ff.; 197b 14 ff.), which are always less significant than the "essential" pattern. For Nahmanides, however, nothing is impossible for the Creator, since he transcends nature. What is impossible to an Aristotelian is miraculous for Nahmanides, as for Halevi. The "impossible" in this sense is not only possible but real, and visible in public miracles.

In modern science, as developed since the times of Copernicus, Galileo and Newton, entities are no longer treated as having innate natures or essences or as parts of unalterable species. Rather, all entities are actual or potential data. Their interrelations in space-time are subject to mathematical quantification, from which causal patterns are abstracted. Since things are no longer seen as having inherent essential properties, the idea of intrinsic impossibility has lost its standing. The only impossibility still universally recognized is logical impossibility, and even that has developed in new ways at the hands of logicians like Alfred North Whitehead and Bertrand Russell, who were heavily influenced by the great developments in modern science. Phenomena not now explainable within an intelligible paradigm may be explainable once an appropriate paradigm is constituted, with the expansion of our experience. The greatest example of such an expansion in this century is Einstein's constituting a new paradigm – the Theory of Special Relativity – to explain phenomena not explained by Newtonian Mechanics. See T. S. Kuhn, *The Structure of Scientific Revolutions* [Chicago: University of Chicago Press, 1962] 43 ff.; and for the indefinite expansibility of experience, David Hume, *A Treatise of Human Nature* I 3.14, ed. L. A. Selby-Bigge [Oxford: Clarendon Press, 1888] 170-72).)

Given the expansion of the idea of possibility in natural science, Nahmanides' distinction between secret and public miracles becomes implausible in the context of the reigning paradigms in natural science today. But his theory of secret miracles remains plausible. For here a miracle is an event in historical time-space rather than an occurrence in physical space-time. Its significance lies in *when* the event happened, to *whom* it happened, and *who* now appreciates it. Only then is *where* it happened of significance. (For the primacy of time-space over space-time in classical Jewish thought, see my late revered teacher, Abraham Joshua Heschel, *The Sabbath*, exp. ed. [New York: Farrar, Straus, 1963], Appendix: "Space, Time and Reality: The Centrality of Time in the Biblical World View." I thank Fritz Rothschild for this reference.)

Historical time-space cannot be understood in nearly as deterministic a way as physical space-time, even for philosophers who see natural patterns in history. Besides, Evolutionary Theory in biology and Quantum Theory in physics address statistical probabilities rather than strict causal laws (see Bernard Lonergan, *Insight*, 3rd ed. [New York: Philosophical Library, 1970], 97 ff.). So most of contemporary natural science does not contradict the possibility of unique events, not predetermined systemically. But a miracle needs only *one lone* event which is not systemically predetermined. Thus there is no longer an unbridgable gap between natural science and spiritual insight. Nahmanides' theory of secret miracles – expanded and adapted to be sure – allows us to develop a theology in which God can be appreciated as both the Creator of the physical universe and the Lord of history.

One can even maintain Nahmanides' distinction between secret and public miracles, if one takes secret miracles as individual experiences of God's special care and public miracles as collective experiences of that same care. Since language is public, the language used by the community in transmitting the memory of its collective experience of God's care can enable individuals to perceive and express their own private miracles in the context of the community in which people speak a shared language of faith (see Max Kadushin, *The Rabbinic Mind* [New York: JTS, 1952] 216-17). For Nahmanides public miracles presuppose secret miracles. But in the view I have just proposed, individual miracles presuppose collective miracles. For the recollection of the latter provides the language for the intelligibility of the former.

[4.4] Hidden miracles mark the distinction between God's general providence, evident in the natural order as a whole, and his special providence, seen only in the lives of the righteous and those who share their faith:

> The Lord's knowledge, which is his providence in the world here below (*ba-'olam ha-shafal*), serves to protect the species. And for that reason even humans can fall victim to particular vicissitudes (*miqrim*)... but with his saints (*hasidav*), he directs conscious attention to them individually, making his care for them continual. His knowledge and mindfulness never depart from them. [CT: Gen. 18:19 - I, 111]

[4.5] For Nahmanides, providence is what explains the commandments and the rewards and punishments in the Torah. Thus, in his reading of the book of Job, Elihu, not Job, is the hero, since his affirmation of providence is the most forceful and consistent of all the positions presented. Nahmanides calls Elihu "the greatest of Job's friends in wisdom" (KR: *Commentary on Job* 22:1 - I, 76). His teaching is cogent, but "not because Elihu has any compelling proof (*r'ayah mukhrahat*). For no one can resolve this issue except by way of tradition (*be-derekh qabbalah*)." [KR: *Commentary on Job* 38:1 - I, 115]

Nahmanides continually makes this point:

> Belief in the omniscience of God, exalted be he, is something clear and evident... [God's knowledge] of the classes of things and of particular individuals is a cornerstone of the Torah of Moses our master... Given this affirmation, the Torah and the commandments endure. For once we believe that God knows and is provident, our faith will extend to prophecy, and we will believe that He, exalted be he, knows and cares, commands and admonishes: He commands us to do what is good and right, admonishes us about what is evil; he will watch over us and maintain for us all the goods promised in the Torah, and will bring all the retributions on those who transgress against what he decreed for them. [KR: *Commentary on Job*, intro. - I, 17-18]

[4.6] Nahmanides speaks of God's de novo creation of the world, knowledge of the world, and providence over it as the three foundations (*mosdot*) of the Torah. [KR: *Torat ha-Shem Temimah* - I, 155].

[4.7] He asserts that nature cannot explain why certain things happen to people because of their merit or fault. The moral significance of such happenings can be explained only in the context of direct divine causality in miracles:

> There is no difference between what the prayers of David son of Jesse accomplish and what our own prayers or any miracles accomplish. For if one said, it is by nature that God nourishes all, then no one would die or live because of merit or fault... On the contrary, all these things are enduring miracles that change the course of natural coming-to-be and alter the power of the exalted constellations in heaven and on earth... all these things are continuous miraculous portents (*moftim qayyamim*). [KR: *Commentary on Job*, intro. - I, 18-19]

[4.8] The patriarch Jacob is assured of the crucial distinction between individual and general providence in his vision:

> God showed him in a dream that everything done on earth is done by means of the angels and at the decree of the Most High in their regard... Yet he assured Jacob with a mighty assurance that he would not be in the hands of the angels, but would be the Lord's own portion. [CT: Gen. 28:12 - I, 157]

[4.9] Hidden miracles are not recorded in the Torah like the miracles publicly anticipated by the prophets. For these continuous miracles are the very foundation of the Torah. They show that keeping the Torah has consequences far beyond the confines of the natural world. For the Torah is founded on the principle that all events belong to the purposeful plan of God. There is no blind chance. If the Torah were simply part of nature, there would be nothing unique or desirable about the relationship of Israel with God. It would be a relationship limited to worldly possibilities, but it would not and could not be a relationship with a loving Father. Thus, for Nahmanides, nature remains in the background. What is vital is Israel's awareness of the presence of God, which is fostered only by the Torah:

> The miracles performed by a prophet who foretold it, or by an angel who appeared on a mission from the Lord, are recorded by Scripture. But those performed to help a righteous person or to destroy a wicked person are not recorded in the Torah or the Prophets... All the foundations (*yesodot*) of the Torah are found in secret miracles, not in nature or the realm of the customary (*ha-minhag*). For the events foretold (*ye'udei*) by the Torah do not manifest any change in the nature of the world. [CT: Gen. 46:15 - I, 254]

[4.10] The supernatural foundation of the Torah is a constant theme:

> When we carefully inquire, we see that no one has a portion in the Torah of Moses our master, peace be upon him, until he believes that all our words and deeds, *all of them*, are miracles. Nothing of nature or the ordinary pertains to them. For all the requitals of the Torah (*ye'udei ha-Torah*) are absolute portents (*moftim gemurim*) [of divine power]. [KR: *Torat ha-Shem Temimah* - I, 153]

[4.11] The "events designated to happen by the Torah" are the promised rewards and punishments of obedience or disobedience to its commandments. The requital demands the operation of secret miracles in the world:

> For all of the events designated in the Torah by promises and warnings are demonstrable from the secret miracles... Thus the Torah warns here about *karet* ["excision"], a miraculous subject (*'inyan nissi*). But it does not assure us here about ordinary survival (*qiyyum*), which is something expected (*ra'uy*). [CT: Lev. 18:29 - II, 114]

The exact meaning of *karet* is much debated (B. Mo'ed Qatan 28a re Deut. 31:14 and Tos. s.v. *mitah*), but it seems to involve a miraculous incursion of God's power into the world, perhaps involving an untimely death.

[4.12] All public miracles serve ultimately to call our attention to God's act of creation. But the secret miracles, being consequences of our observing God's commandments, mark our sharing in God's life:

> It has already been made clear that public miracles teach the creation of the world de novo, God's knowledge of particulars, and his providence. But the secret miracles teach what every believer should know about the punishment of sins and the reward for keeping the commandments. [KR: *Torat ha-Shem Temimah* - I, 155]

[4.13] The linkage between the pious and God's unseen miracles is merit. These miracles are performed by God for the pious because they deserve them. By their meritorious deeds, then, the pious share with God in his creative and providential activity. The lives of the patriarchs are archetypes of this process:

> God appeared to the patriarchs by this name which indicates that he is the One who vanquishes the heavenly configurations and performs great miracles for them... but the full reward for keeping the Torah and punishment for transgressing it are miracles that are secret. One who sees them might think them part of the familiar world order, although in truth they are punishments or rewards for an individual. [CT: Exod. 6:2 - I, 303]

[4.14] The term *sod* has two senses: It refers to what God reveals to the prophets of his plans, or to God's caring for those who are faithful to him:

> "As I was in the days of my vigor when God was an intimate (*be-sod*) in my tent" (Job 29:4) means roughly the same as "the Lord's *sod* is made known to those who fear him." (Psalms 25:14)... He says that the divine mystery is known in his tent, as if he were prophesying future events... or... it could

> mean that the heavenly angels and hosts were abiding over his tent to protect him from all harm. [KR: *Commentary on Job* 29:4 - I, 90]

Sod pertains to the secret miracles in both senses. The miracles protect the righteous, and the righteous have prophet-like knowledge of their true significance.

[4.15] Human beings seem wholly dependent on physical nature because they have lost the grace to transcend it – most pointedly, to transcend death:

> According to the opinion of the naturalists (*anshei ha-teva*), man is subject (*me'uttar*) to death from the beginning of his formation (*ha-yetsirah*) because he is composite... But the determination of death is in the hands of God... [and it is that human beings] must die because of their sin before their time. [CT: Gen. 2:17 - I, 37]

For further discussion, see KR: *Torat ha-'Adam*: Sha'ar ha-Gemul - II, 274, where Nahmanides elaborates on the rabbinic doctrine that human death is not the inevitable result of general biological nature, but of specifically human sin (B. Shabbat 55a-b). It is sin that makes us mortal like the rest of creation. Thus neither before nor after the expulsion from Eden is the human lifespan natural. Before the expulsion, humans were to live forever. Their immortality was a chief distinction from the animals. After the expulsion, our lifespan was diminished further. For virtually all human beings die because of their individual sins, not because of their biological constitution. For the difference between general and individual mortality, the first being inherited from Adam and Eve, the second acquired by the desert of each individual, see KR: *Disputation*, no. 45 - I, 310.

[4.16] Obedience to the commandments does not require the secret miracles as a precondition. One is not to wait for such a miracle before performing a commandment of the Torah. Nahmanides here applies the rabbinic dictum that "one is not to rely on miracles" (B. Shabbat 32a; B. Pesahim 64b; B. Ta'anit 20b) in any specific case. As he puts it, "Torah does not depend on miracles, for example, that one will pursue a thousand" [CT: Num. 1:45 - II, 199]. Rather, the secret miracles are the promised general consequence of keeping the commandments properly. Without such observance, these miracles would not be performed at all. Indeed, one can say that the very purpose of the commandments is to ensure that the secret miracles are deserved. For their occurrence is not just for the gratification of the keeper of the commandments but, more crucially, to make us aware of the presence and power of God:

> The revelation of God's presence (*gilui Shekhinah*) here and elsewhere was not to issue a commandment or any communication at all, but as a reward for the performance of the commandment already fulfilled. [CT: Gen. 18:1 - I, 106]

[4.17] Only in rare cases is there any overt entailment of a miracle. Such a case is the punishment the Torah mentions for the woman publicly accused of adultery (*sotah*) without eyewitnesses to the act. If she manifests physical affliction after undergoing the Ordeal of the Bitter Waters, this is considered miraculous:

> Indeed, there is nothing in any of the humanly applicable laws (*mishpetei*) of the Torah that is contingent on a miracle except this one. It is a marvel (*pele*), a permanent miracle. It is a miracle wrought in the Land of Israel in times when most of the people are doing the will of God... The general principle is that this is a miracle performed as a signal honor in behalf of Israel. [CT: Num. 5:20 - II, 214-15]

There is also direct supernatural involvement in the commandment pertaining to the infection of houses in the Land of Israel (see CT: Lev. 13:47 - II, 75).

[4.18] The patriarchs were the first recipients of secret miracles, as a result of keeping those commandments that were given to them. In the case of Moses greater miracles were called for, since the Torah was to be given through him:

> What came to the patriarchs was a revelation of God's presence (*gilui Shekhinah*). God's speech with them was by means of the weak attribute of justice... But with Moses, God acted and made himself known through the attribute of mercy, which is his Great Name... and the Torah was given through his Great Name. [CT: Exod. 6:2 - I, 304]

[4.19] The commandments which occasion the secret miracles presuppose nothing miraculous in itself. They prescribe actions to be performed in the natural world in an ordinary way. What is miraculous is that the outcomes of these actions benefit particular human beings in particular ways:

> For the Torah commands naturalistically (*be-derekh erets*) and God performs miracles in secret for those who fear him. For it is not his wish to change the nature of the world, except where there is no other way to save. [CT: Deut. 20:9 - II, 435]

[4.20] Human beings in general must accomplish as much as they can by ordinary means. Only when these reach their inherent limits does supernatural action take over:

> So it is with all the miracles in the Torah or the Prophets: What can be done by man is done by man and the rest is in the hand of God. [CT: Gen. 6:9 - I, 54]

For "man is not exalted and saved by his own power, but only because the Most High watches over him" [CT: Gen. 4:13 - I, 45].

[4.21] It follows from the idea of a miraculous reward that one must not see any ordinary humanly attainable goals as the raison d'etre of the commandments. These are only the most immediate results of following the commandments. The ultimate rewards promised by the Torah are far beyond ordinary expectation:

> It is not the Lord's will to perform miracles for everyone at all times... But you must keep His statutes even though you do not know their reason. For in fact, God will benefit you in the end. [CT: Deut. 6:16 - II, 376]

[4.22] Secret miracles are perfromed for extraordinary people; ordinary people live mostly within the realm of ordinary nature.

> For the Lord will not continually perform miracles... and you must know that miracles are performed, whether for good or for harm, only for the altogether righteous or the altogether wicked. For ordinary people (*ha-beinonim*), things proceed according to the normal course of events in the world (*minhago shel 'olam*) [CT: Deut. 11:13 - II, 393]

[4.23] There are two ways of coming to appreciate secret miracles: from above and from below. From above, faith in the efficacy of God's power and providence can enable one to see them at work in the world. But such faith is attained only by a few gifted individuals. Most people have to learn the significance of secret miracles from below. That is, they have to be startled out of complacent acceptance of the world's running according to its accustomed ways. This jolting experience is the purpose of public miracles (*nissim mefursamim*):

> Out of the experience of the great public miracles a person will come to acknowledge the secret miracles, which are the foundation (*yesod*) of the entire Torah. For no one has a portion in the Torah of Moses our master unless he believes

> that eveything that happens to us (*khol devareinu u-miqreinu*), everything, is a miracle. There is nothing natural or ordinary about it, whether it pertains to many people or only to one individual... And thus will the [reality of] secret miracles become publicized in the eyes of many people as their occurrence is predicted by the Torah (*be-yi'udei ha-Torah*) in its blessings and curses... So will it become published to all the nations that what befalls them is their punishment from the Lord. [CT: Exod. 13:16 - I, 346-47]

[4.24] Although the secret miracles underlie the public miracles in reality, it is because of the public miracles that we can appreciate the constant possibility of the secret miracles.

> For the public miracles teach of God's creation of the world (*ha-hiddush*) and his omniscience as to individuals in the world – thus about providence. But the secret miracles serve to make known to every believer the punishment of sins and the reward for keeping the commandments, so that everyone who prays and lifts up his eyes to heaven will sincerely acknowledge God's act of creation, omniscience and providence. [KR: *Torat ha-Shem Temimah* - I, 155]

In *Sefer ha-'Emunah ve-ha-Bitahon*, thought to be by a theologian of Nahmanides' school (see Chavel's introduction, KR, II, 341 ff.), a critical distinction is made between belief (*emunah*) and trust (*bitahon*) as types of faith. Belief is cognitive, acceptance of the doctrines of Judaism, especially individual providence. Trust is practical, attitudinal, a certitude as to God's providence over oneself. The difference reflects Nahmanides' distinction between secret and public miracles: Belief is engendered by public miracles; trust, by the secret miracles. And belief is for the sake of trust (*ibid.*, 355-56), just as the public miracles are for the sake of the secret miracles.

[4.25] Wonder and suprise open the way to the experience of God's presence. This fact is underscored by Nahmanides in a charged etymology:

> 'Demonstration' (*mofet*) is the term designating something new done before us by changing the nature of the world... This word is a contraction of 'wonderous' (*mufla'et*).... The Hebrew language adapted its meaning to designate something extraordinary (*huts min ha-minhag*)... for all its events are wonderous (*pele*) in the eyes of those who behold them. [CT: Deut. 13:2 - II, 404-05]

[4.26] The continuum between secret and public miracles is seen in Nahmanides' use of the rabbinic expression 'miracle within a miracle' (*nes be-tokh nes* - B. Shabbat 97a and parallels).

> It is the assumption of the Torah that all its events (*ma'aseiha*) are miracles within miracles... the idea is that the Lord commanded that they be healed with what would normally harm them... to let them know that it is the Lord who kills and who restores to life. [CT: Num. 21:9 - II, 283-84]

Nahmanides sees an "inner miracle" in God's healing of the rebellious people who were bitten by snakes. The "outer miracle" is that their cure was brought about in a way totally at variance with ordinary human experience and expectations. The accepted medical opinion, as the Talmud indicates (B. Yoma 84a), Nahmanides argues, would lead one to expect that a victim of snakebite would be traumatized by having to gaze at the image of the very creature that caused the suffering. Yet that was the vehicle of the cure. Encapsulated in this public miracle, was the inner, unseen miracle, God's secret healing of those who obeyed his commandment.

Nahmanides' account may seem to endorse the idea that there were magical properties in the brazen serpent Moses made and held up in front of the people (Num. 21:9). But his closing words, that it is God who "kills and restores to life" (echoing Deut. 32:39) are clearly meant to dispel such a reading. Nahmanides' concern to dispel any suggestion here of the efficacy of magic follows both Scriptural (II Kings 18:4) and rabbinic traditions (M. Rosh Hashanah 3.8; cf. B. Yevamot 6a-b re Lev. 19:30; Maimonides, *Hilkhot Shehitah*, 14.16).

[4.27] Public miracles are evidence of the greatest miracle, that of creation. Bringing being from absolute non-being is unthinkable without the direct action of God. But once the act of creation is over, the familiar order of nature seems to take over, and the natural world appears to be self-contained and self-sufficient. Public miracles shatter this illusion and point beyond themselves to the ever present power of the Creator. The paradigm of all such miracles is the Exodus. In explaining why the Exodus is mentioned in the prologue to the Ten Commandments, Nahmanides writes:

> It also teaches about the creation of the world de novo (*ha-hiddush*). For if the world were eternal (*qadmut ha-'olam*), nothing could alter its nature. [CT: Exod. 20:2 - I, 388]

[4.28] Participation in the Exodus is a more immediate foundation for keeping the commandments than any abstract reason drawn from ordinary experience.

> For the Lord is the Creator, the Will and the Power (*ha-yekholet*), as was made clear to us at the Exodus from Egypt. This is the reason (*ta'am*) present before our eyes. [CT: Deut. 6:20 - II, 377]

Nahmanides is heavily indebted here to Halevi (*Kuzari*, 1.25). Tradition, as the record of God's mighty acts in history, supplies the most complete information about God available to human beings.

[4.29] Writing about the miracle of the earth opening to swallow Korah and his rebellious band, Nahmanides asserts:

> The earth's splitting open is not literally a new creation. But the opening of its mouth to swallow is an unprecedented novum (*hiddush*)... that event was made anew that very day as if (*ke'ilu*) created from nothing. [CT: Num. 16:30 - II, 263]

Elsewhere Nahmanides states: "great miracle is like a new creation" (CT: Num. 22:23 - II, 291).

[4.30] The Exodus, as the paradigm of all public miracles, is the vital link between the creation of the world and the revelation of the Torah at Mount Sinai. For according to the laws about prophecy, miracles are to be accepted as valid signs only when the message that accompanies them is consistent with the commandments of the Torah. Otherwise, the that message is invalid, regardless how impressive the event:

> Scripture commanded us not to listen to anyone who prophesies in the name of the Lord to worship idols. We should pay no attention to the signs and portents he produces. It gives the reason: We know by the Exodus from Egypt, which is a real event (*ma'aseh mamash*), not a vision or a spectre, that the earth is his and he is the Creator, the Will and the Power – there is no God but he. And we know from the revelation at Mount Sinai, which was face to face, that he commanded us to walk in this way and serve none but him. [CT: Deut. 13:2 - II, 405-06]

Maimonides too emphasizes the uniqueness of God's self-revelation at Sinai as the basis for the commandment to listen to no prophet who orders the people of Israel to practice idolatry, even temporarily (*Hilkhot Yesodei ha-Torah*, 8.2-3; 9.5; cf. *Hilkhot Mamrim*, 2.4). But in Maimonides the prohibition of idolatry is not grounded in historical experience, not even in Sinai. For him Sinai is the strongest confirmation of the falsity of idolatry, which he insists is self-evident (*muskal*) to any rational person (*Moreh*, 2.33).

Its prohibition is a matter of natural law, essentially transhistorical. But for Nahmanides the historical experience is the foundation.

[4.31] Public miracles awaken people from disbelief, less through direct experience than through reenactment:

> The great miracles serve to silence those of little faith. They are not performed in every generation, either because the generations do not deserve them or because there is no need for them. So God commanded us to establish a perpetual reminder of these miracles, and was very insistent about it... For you have been a witness to a divine creative act (*ha-hiddush*), make a perpetual memorial of it, to remember always and make known publicly that he is the Creator of the world, who watches over his creatures providently, benefitting those who perform his will, and punishing those who transgress it. [KR: *Torat ha-Shem Temimah* - I, 151]

[4.32] Sinai is central. Miracles experienced by individuals are for its sake. The Exodus and the revelation at Sinai were experienced by the whole people of Israel. No other miracle before or since was so absolutely public:

> And in the manner of deeper truth, the words "this is for you a sign"... say: I will be with you; and the sign for you is indeed the sign of the covenant, attesting that I will be with you forever... For I send you [Moses] that they shall serve God on this mountain and then I shall ascend in the midst of this people to the place I have prepared [for them]. [CT: Exod. 3:12 - I, 290]

[4.33] The public miracles, epitomized by Exodus-Sinai, break down resistance to God's commandments. For when the customary order of the world is publicly upset, the order of the commandments stands as the sole alternative to give structure to our lives. Referring to the dictum that God tested Israel at Sinai, Nahmanides writes:

> This is literally a trial, in that God wanted to test whether we would keep his commandments, so he removed from our hearts every doubt. Henceforth he will see whether we desire him and his commandments. [CT: Exod. 20:20 - I, 407]

[4.34] Those most likely to be affected by public miracles are those who have no more reason to trust in political powers than to trust in natural powers:

"For I see the tears of the oppressed who have no comforter and no strength to be released from the hand of their oppressors" [Ecclesiastes 4:1]... For I will hear their cry, since these poor people have no confidence (*'einam bot'him*) in their own lives, but can trust only me. [CT: Exod. 22:20 - I, 435]

Chapter 5

The Natural and the Supernatural

[5.1] Nahmanides states repeatedly that the Torah is based on secret miracles, but he does not scorn nature (see, e.g., CT: Lev. 23:17 - II, 150). Christianity, he argues, upholds the impossible, God becoming man. But Judaism advocates only the supernatural:

> What you believe as the very root of your faith is unacceptable to reason. It is something nature does not allow, and the prophets never proclaimed... that the Creator of heaven and earth... would become a fetus in the womb of a Jewish woman... and then grow up and be handed over to his enemies, who sentence him to death and execute him, and that he then return to his former state. Neither Jewish nor universal reason can accept this. [KR: *Disputation*, sec. 5 - I, 311]

[5.2] Nahmanides' view of miracles, secret or public, is not a version of the occasionalism developed by some Islamic theologians, as Gershom Scholem and others after him have supposed (*Ha-Kabbalah be-Gerona*, 309-10). The theory is ably put to rest by David Berger, "Miracles and the Natural Order in Nahmanides" in Twersky, ed., *Rabbi Moses Nahmanides:* 114-16.)

Occasionalism denies the internal connectedness of nature altogether, making every event the immediate and particular outcome of God's choices. If occasionalism were true, there would be nothing special about revelation, since everything would be a miracle. (For the necessity of a natural order as a backdrop for miracles, see Judah Loewe [Maharal], *Gevurot ha-Shem* [Cracow, 1582], 2nd intro. and ch. 61 re B. Shabbat 118b.)

Nahmanides clearly affirms a continuity within nature. The world is created by God, but then operates on its own internal principles. These do not immediately reflect the singular choices of God but generally sustain their godgiven natural pattern. Rather than oppose the idea of nature, Nahmanides opposes only the claim of the rationalist theologians of his time that nature is the meeting ground for God and man. Specifically, he opposes Aristotelian claims that nature is unalterable, based on the observed regularity of nature. His rejection of the naturalism of his day resembles the growing rejection of scientism today, the view that the natural sciences provide the only avenue to truth about the human condition. In emphasizing this point, Nahmanides sometimes seems to deny the reality of the natural order altogether:

> Let not a man believe, along with belief in the Torah, in the subsistence of nature at all. For everything is miraculous (*be-nissim*). That is why the Torah elaborates on consequences which are outside nature. [KR: *Sermon on Kohelet* - I, 192]

[5.3] But usually Nahmanides avoids such hyperbole. He held that the secret miracles are rare and are not a substitute for the natural order. Yet he differed from Maimonides about that order. He held astrology and even demonology to be natural sciences. For Maimonides, they are dangerous, forbidden superstitions (esp., *Hilkhot 'Avodah Zarah*, 11.8-9, 11, 16; "Letter to the Sages of Montpelier" in *Igrot ha-Rambam*, ed. Y. Shailat [Jerusalem: Ma'aliyot, 1988] 2.478 ff.) The disagreement reflects the divergent epistemologies of the two thinkers. These stem in turn from their divergent ontologies. In Maimonides' view, natural science knows what is presently demonstrable; history is the record of the unrepeatable past and is not in itself the source of any independent truth (see D. Novak, "Does Maimonides Have A Philosophy of History?" in N. M. Samuelson, ed. *Studies in Jewish Philosophy*, 397 ff.) In Nahmanides' view, however, history, in the form of tradition, is ultimately more reliable than scientific demonstration. Since astral influences and demons are taken seriously by rabbinic tradition, Nahmanides refuses to dismiss them from the realm of the natural.

Yet he does exclude them from the realm of the miraculous, which alone enables us to experience God's sovereignty and providence directly. By confining astrology and demonology to the realm of the natural, Nahmanides disenchants them without dismissing their presumed utility:

> It is certain that astrology (*ha-'itstagninut*) is not in the [prohibited] category of divination (*nihush*)... R. Hanina thought that one's constellation (*mazal*) makes one rich and that Israel has its own constellation. Even though this view is not followed halakhically, we are given to understand that [believing in the power of the constellations] is not divination... We learn that Abraham said, "I have gained insight (*nistakalti*) through astrology"...

> Sometimes God performs a miracle for those who fear him, by annulling a decree of the stars. Such acts belong to the category of hidden miracles, which are performed through the workings of nature (*be-derekh tashmisho shel 'olam*). The whole Torah depends on these. One does not ask for them, but carries on in faithful simplicity (*be-temimut*)...
>
> If one sees by means of [the various forms of astrology] something inimical to his own desire, let him fulfill more commandments and pray more. But if one saw by way of astrology that a certain day is not propitious for his work, he should avoid it and not count on a miracle by running in the face of a decree of the constellations.
>
> Maimonides wrote that whoever performs an act because of astrology or schedules his work or travel at times determined by the astrologers (*hovrei shamayim*), is subject to flogging for violating the prohibition, "you shall not practice soothsaying" (Lev. 19:26 - *Hilkhot 'Avodah Zarah*, 1.9). He added that such beliefs are foolish and stupid... But many passages in the Talmud and Midrash incline to accept them. [*Hiddushei ha-Ramban ha-Shalem*: B. Shabbat 156b, pp. 519-20]

Maimonides' objection to astrology was not only intellectual. He was opposed to it on moral grounds, because it denies free choice, which Maimonides regards as a necessary presupposition of the whole system of commandments (*Hilkhot Teshuvah*, 5.4).

For the recognition of the influence of the constellations in ordinary experience, see Nahmanides's chief disciple, Solomon ibn Adret, *Responsa Rashba* I, no. 141; *Responsa Rashba Attributed to Nahmanides*, no. 285. From the later Nahmanidean school, see Rabbenu Bahya ben Asher, *Commentary on the Torah*: Deut. 8:18.

[5.4] Nahmanides considered astrology a science accurately reflecting the workings of nature. Since the hidden miracles are rewards of God's grace, one must never rely on them before acting. One should assume only what is customarily the case, including what is taken to be the case by means of astrology. Such assumptions are not part of the proscribed "ways of the Amorites" (see M. Shabbat 6.10). In a responsum Nahmanides both demonstrates and qualifies rabbinic precedents for astrology and magic (*Teshuvot ha-Ramban*, no. 104, pp. 152-57). He concludes by designating most of these precedents aggadah.

When Maimonides distinguishes between science and superstition (*Commentary on the Mishnah*: Pesahim 4.10), he places astrology on the side of superstition. In this respect Nahmanides' concept of science is wider than that of Maimonides; the natural order includes more for him than it does for Maimonides.

[5.5] Consistent with his respect for nature, Nahmanides explains a number of prohibitions of the Torah as showing deference to the integrity of nature:

> When the Creator, exalted be he, created everything from nothing, he made the higher beings (*ha-'elyonim*) govern (*manhigei*) the lower beings beneath them... but the simple direction in this process is the will of the Creator, exalted be he, who primordially (*me-'az*) gave them such power. This is the mystery of sorcery and its power... which can confound the heavenly retinue (*pamalya*)... Thus it is right for the Torah to forbid it so as to let the world function according to its regular custom and its simple nature, which is the will of the Creator. This is also one of the reasons for the prohibition of mixing species of plants (*kil'ayim*), for plants from such graftings will function strangely, producing what is different from the normal order of the world. [CT: Deut. 18:9 - II, 427]

Maimonides considered sorcery a delusion, with no real effect on the world. For Nahmanides, sorcery does have a real effect. It can be a powerful form of technology, as he believes experience often shows. It is objectionable on theological, not ontological, grounds, as an unwarranted tampering with nature, an example of our forgetting our place in the created order.

[5.6] Although Nahmanides acknowledges a natural order, unlike the rationalist, Aristotelian theologians, he does not regard that order as commensurate with human reason. Thus even respect for the *natural* order cannot be left to human reason alone. It requires revelation. For example, crossbreeding is forbidden because it violates the natural order. But one would not know this unless informed by revelation. Thus, in commenting on the verse, "You shall keep my statutes (*et huqqotai*): you shall not crossbreed species" (Lev. 19:19), Nahmanides notes:

> The *huqqim* are the King's decree (*gezerat ha-melekh*), which he ordained in his kingdom without revealing their utility (*to'eletam*) to the people... One who crossbreeds species changes and denies (*u-makh'heesh*) the very work of creation, as if he thought that God did not adequately fulfill (*she-lo hishlim*) every need. [CT: Lev. 19:19 - II, 120]

See B. Sanhedrin 56b, Tos., s.v. *le-minehu*; Novak, *The Image of the Non-Jew in Judaism*, 244-48.

[5.7] In preserving the distinction between the natural and the supernatural yet insisting on the reality of both, Nahmanides reiterates a doctrine found in the Hellenistic and Rabbinic traditions (see LXX on Deut. 32:8; Siracides 17:17; B. Shabbat 156a), that the nations of the world are all under secondary and predetermined cosmic powers, whereas Israel is under the free and direct providence of God. The secondary powers are the equivalent of what philosophers call "nature." Like these semi-autonomous heavenly beings, Israel has no intermediary between herself and God:

> And he commanded that the judges of Israel be this number seventy... For Israel are the armies (*tsiv'ot*) of the Lord on earth... Their number is like the number of the heavenly officers (*sarei ma'alah*). [CT: Num. 11:16 - II, 233-34]

[5.8] Rule depends on how close a being is to the ultimate source of all authority in God:

> Rulership (*memshalah*) is the further power of emanation (*atsilut*). The higher beings govern (*manhigei*) the lower, and it is by their power that everything which rules rules... as it is written, "which [sc., the power of the heavenly bodies] the Lord alloted to all the peoples" [Deut. 4:19]... according to the mystical way (*derekh ha-sod*) I have hinted to you, they are truly to have complete rule. [CT: Gen. 1:18 - I, 23]

Deut. 4:19 is read as stating that the heavenly bodies may be worshipped by the gentiles but not by Israel because of her direct, covenantal relationship with God. It gives no ontological reason for the apparent permission to other nations. But the reason supplied by tradition is that the gentile nations are under the rule of these heavenly bodies, by God's decree.

[5.9] Idolatry means approaching God through such cosmic intermediaries:

> Those who sacrifice to his angels think they are performing his will, because these angels are intermediaries (*emtsa'im*) who can draw his will to them. [CT: Exod. 22:19 - I, 434]

[5.10] Idolatry is the way of the gentiles, who are bereft of God's direct revelation in the Torah. Strikingly, Nahmanides does not invoke the Rabbinic doctrine of the Seven Noahide Commandments, where idolatry is prohibited to gentiles, as it is to Jews (B. Sanhedrin 56b re Gen. 2:16). He is followed by his disciple, Solomon ibn Adret and by Bahya ben Asher (see *She'elot u-Teshuvot ha-Rashba* IV, 334; Rabbenu Bahya, *Commentary on the Torah*: Deut. 31:15; see *The Image of the Non-Jew in Judaism*, 111 ff.):

> The first humans began to serve the angels, viz., the disembodied intelligences, because it was known to some that they hold dominion (*serarah*) over the nations... They thought that these beings have the power to cause benefit and harm... even though those who served them acknowledged that the

> greatest power and most complete competence belong to the supreme (*'elyon*) God. [CT: Exod. 22:19 - I, 392]

Maimonides, by contrast, emphasizes the universality of the prohibition against idolatry (*Commentary on the Mishnah*: 'Avodah Zarah 4.7; *Hilkhot 'Avodah Zarah*, 1.1 ff.).

[5.11] According to Nahmanides, idolatry is not sinful (at least as far as Scripture is concerned) for gentiles as long as it is recognized as esentially symbolic, ultimately intending the Maker of heaven and earth, approaching the supreme God, as it were, by way of intermediaries (cf. B. Sanhedrin 63b, Tos. s.v. *assur*; Ibn Gabirol, "Keter Malkhut", sec. 8). Such idolatry is proscribed only for those who are the direct recipients of revelation.

> I have already explained "those which the Lord your God allotted to all the nations" [Deut. 4:19]: For each nation there is a star and a constellation, and above these are the angels of the Most High... That is why they make gods for themselves to rule over them and they serve them. He [Moses] said, "for the Lord took you" [Deut. 4:20] because you are the portion of the Lord and you shall not set up over yourselves any heavenly authority (*sar*) or helper (*'ozer*) except him. [CT: Deut. 4:15- II, 362-63]

[5.12] Outside the context of revelation, idolatry can even be seen as honoring God:

> Most idolators grasp and understand that the Lord (glory be to him) is God of gods (*elohim*) and Lord of Lords. Their intent in idol worship derives only from the notion that they will benefit further by serving the angels, since they are honoring the ministers of the great God. [CT: Exod. 23:25 - I, 444]

[5.13] In an extraordinary comment on the Torah's commandment to send a goat to "Azazel" on Yom Kippur, Nahmanides finds an acknowledgement of lesser powers, even though this rite is emphatically not worship of them:

> This is the mystical meaning (*sod*) of the act: ...although the Torah cateorically forbids any acceptance of their divinity or service to them, God still commanded that on Yom Kippur we should send a goat into the wilderness, to the magistrate (*sar*) who holds dominion over places of desolation... The intention in sending the goat is not that it be a sacrifice from us – God forbid! Rather, our intent must be to do the will of our Creator, who so commanded us – like one who prepared a meal

> for his master, who in turn ordered him to give a portion to a certain servant of his. The one who prepares the meal does gives no honor to that servant in his own right... he acts only out of deference to his master... because the master wanted all his servants to enjoy that meal... This is why lots are cast [to distinguish the goats]. For if the priest actually consecrated the goats to the Lord and Azazel, it would be tantamount to serving Azazel and dedicating something to him. But he sets them at the opening of the Tent of Assembly, since both are gifts to the Lord, who allots his servant the portion that comes to him from the Lord. [CT: Lev. 16:8 - II, 88-89]

[5.14] Jewish tradition includes all natural wisdom, but much of it was lost after the destruction of the Temple:

> All these things [various scientific insights] and much that is similar – wisdom ancient and true – were received by those who received the Torah. But when we were undone, this wisdom was lost to us. Its memory remains in a confused state with a few people. But the philosophers came and discredited it... Finally, the Torah hints (*nirmaz*) to the wise about all matters of nature... matters which the physicians (*ha-rof'im*) call first principles, second principles, third principles, and the treasures they contain. [KR: *Torat ha-Shem Temimah* - I, 162]

Maimonides argues similarly (*Shemonah Peraqim*, intro.; *Hilkhot Qiddush ha-Hodesh*, 17.24; *Moreh*, 1.71.), but he holds that the lost wisdom can be regained through natural human thought processes. For Nahmanides, it can be regained only through the retrieval of authentic tradition. He was highly critical of those who attempted to retrieve ancient *Jewish* wisdom by immersing themselves in the works of Greek philosophers (KR: *Letters*, no. 2, I, 339). Once again his approach reveals the influence of Judah Halevi (*Kuzari*, 2.66).

[5.15] Nahmanides' careful distinction between the natural and the supernatural affords the background for his view of medicine. He was himself a physician without apology. But he saw the practice of medicine as confined within the bounds of nature, which the righteous, he believed, could transcend, even ceasing to be dependent on medical treatment altogether. For Nahmanides, medicine is often dangerously misleading, usurping the role of God by seeming to claim complete control. He emphasizes how the infirmities of the righteous were cured by God, without medical intervention. Of Rachel's conception after years of barrenness, he writes, "It was through prayer that Rachel was made to conceive and not by way of human cures (*ha-refu'ot*)" [CT: Gen. 30:14 - I, 168]

Yet as long as medicine is not absolutized, its efficacy is readily acknowledged by Nahmanides. In fact, the ordinary human condition makes medical treatment a necessity, and Nahmanides seems to designate it as a welcome form of *imitatio Dei* – when the physician is aware of the source and limits of his healing powers and sees them as a participation in God's work. He compares the physician's intervention against illness to a judge's intervention against injustice. Both are mandated by the Torah, and the Rabbis emphasize a judge's participation in divine justice (B. Shabbat 10a; B. Sanhedrin 6a *et seq.*). In Nahmanides' view both justice and healing must be *in* the world but not *of* it.

He builds on this point in discussing a rabbinic gloss on Exodus 21:19. Scripture commands: "He shall surely heal (*rappo yerappe*)." The Rabbis report: "It was taught in the School of Rabbi Ishmael... here we learn that the physician is authorized (*she-nittan reshut*) to heal" (B. Baba Kama 85a). The word for authorization here has an unusual force. Usually it denotes something optional (e.g., M. Sotah 8.7; B. Baba Batra 8b; Hullin 105a), or an imperfect obligation (e.g., B. Berakhot 26a and Tos., s.v. *ta'ah*; M. Betsah 5.2 and Rashi and Maimonides *ad loc.*; B. Betsah 36b and Tos., s.v. *ve-ha*; Y. Betsah 5.2 / 63a). Yet here it seems to denote a full obligation. Addressing this unusual usage, Nahmanides presents a theological construction of the role of medicine:

> The explanation of this Talmudic dictum is that the physician might well say, "Why do I need all this trouble; I might err (*et'eh*) and commit manslaughter by my error (*bi-shegagah*)?" So the Torah licenses him (*natnah lo reshut*) to heal... Some say that the physician is like a judge, who is obligated to judge (*metsuveh la-doon*)... And it makes sense... Here permission means a dispensation arising from a mandate (*reshut de-mitsvah*), namely, to heal. It falls under the rubric of life saving (*piquah nefesh*). [KR: *Torat ha-'Adam*: 'Inyan Sakkanah - II, 41-42]

Nahmanides' words "dispensation arising from a mandate (*reshut de-mitsvah*)" come from B. Baba Kama 30a and B. Baba Metsia 118b, where a dispensation (*reshut*) is proposed exempting one from liability for damages if one's Hanukkah lamp happens to ignite the property of someone passing in the street (M. Baba Kama 6.6). A commandment mandates that the lamp be placed at the front of one's house, to proclaim the miracle of Hanukkah (B. Shabbat 21b), although the act involves risks which would normally be forbidden. (For the prohibition [*issur*] of creating a situation dangerous to others' property, over and above liability [*hiyyuv*] for any actual damages, see Maimonides, *Hilkhot Nizqei Mammon*, 5.1 [cf. *Rabad ad loc.*] re B. Baba Kama 23b [cf. Tos., s.v. *hanahu, ad loc.*] and 46a re Deut. 22:8; Nahmanides, *Dinei de-Geramei* in *Hiddushei ha-Ramban ha-Shalem*, ed. M. Hershler [Jerusalem: Makhon ha-Talmud ha-Yisraeli ha-Shalem, 1970], 137, 140 re B.

Baba Batra 22b and *Alfasi ad loc.*) Even though the law in the case of the Hanukkah lamp does not follow the proposed view (see Maimonides, *Hilkhot Nizqei Mammon*, 14.13), Nahmanides borrows the argument that medicine involves a mandate and a corresponding dispensation. Without the commandment to heal, the practice of medicine might be prohibited as an intrusion on God's domain, if not an unwarranted risk.

Maimonides, for his part, does not base the obligation to heal on this Talmudic text. When he does quote Exodus 21:19, he retains its original Scriptural context. Following a different interpretation in the Talmud (B. Baba Kama 84a), he understands the verse as mandating that one who injures another must pay the costs of medical treatment but is not subject to *lex talionis* (*Hilkhot Hovel u-Maziq*, 1.5). In his *Commentary on the Torah*, Nahmanides too reads Exodus 21:19 in this fashion, following the Talmud's ruling (B. Baba Kama 85a) that medical expenses are to be paid directly to the physician rather than to the patient.

Maimonides sees here no general mandate to heal. Rather, the verse presupposes such a mandate, which Maimonides regards as part of a more general mandate to practice benevolence and avoid maleficence (*Commentary on the Mishnah*: Nedarim 4.4 re Deut. 22:2, B. Baba Kama 81b and B. Sanhedrin 73a; *Hilkhot Rotseah*, 1.14 re Lev. 19:16; *Hilkhot Mattnot 'Aniyyim*,8.10; *Hilkhot Evel*, 14.1 re Lev. 19:18). In Maimonides' theology, *imitatio Dei* follows God's universal benevolence in nature, not his special, supernatural benevolence (*Moreh*, 3.23, 3.54), as in Nahmanides. To assign any special, supernatural role to healing would be, for Maimonides, a dangerous compromise with superstition. Healing is part of God's general providence, to be imitated by humans. But its efficacy is governed by the same natural laws that operate throughout creation (*Commentary on the Mishnah*: Pesahim 4.10; 'Avodah Zarah 4.7). Its obligations belong to our general moral duties, not to a special, spiritual affinity of the physician to the Creator and Judge of the universe.

[5.16] For Nahmanides our engagement in the natural order is proportional to our distance from God. So reliance on ordinary medical treatement seems a decline from grace.

> The general principle is that when Israel is perfect and numerous, nature will not apply to them at all, neither in their bodies nor in their land, neither collectively nor individually... They did not need a physician or caution about medical matters, as it says, "For I the Lord am your physician" [Exod. 15:26]. And so did the righteous do during the time of the prophets... The only task of the physicians was to tell people what to eat and drink, and what not... But when they began practicing medicine, the Lord made them subject to the accidents of nature. That is what the sages meant when they said, "'he shall

> surely heal; [Exod. 21:19] – here we learn that the physician is authorized to heal" [B. Baba Kama 85a]. They did not say that the sick person *may* be healed, but that when a patient becomes sick and comes for treatment, since he has grown accustomed to medical treatment, not belonging to the assembly whom the Lord himself designated for life, the physician may not refrain from treating him... He should not say that the Lord alone is the healer of all flesh. For these people have already become accustomed to medicine.... For the Torah did not base its laws (*dineiha*) on miracles. [CT: Lev. 26:11 - II, 185-86]

[5.17] Since most of the commandments of the Torah assume the ordinary state of the natural world, one can identify natural reasons for them in addition to the supernatural ones. Nahmanides objects to the assignment of naturalistic reasons when such rationales seem to limit the commandments to a naturalistic aim. But if reductionism is avoided, he is more than willing to employ naturalistic interpretations himself:

> Indeed, the reason for forbidding birds of prey is the savagery of their kind... Moreover, in permitted fowl there is an obvious hygienic (*ha-refu'ot*) benefit. [CT: Lev. 11:13 - II, 58]

[5.18] The realm of nature is one of strict justice, where consequences are meted out in exact proportion to the tenor of human acts. This is the theological basis of Nahmanides' affirmation of natural law. But the realm of miraculous providence is one of mercy. Here consequences are out of proportion to our acts, and generosity is not merely natural but abundantly gracious. Yet, even here, justice is not obliterated but only transcended at its outer limit:

> For I know him [Abraham] as one who recognizes and knows that I the Lord love charity (*tsedaqah*) and justice (*mishpat*), that I do justice only charitably (*bi-tsedaqah*). Therefore, he will command his children and household after him to uphold his way. [CT: Gen. 18:17 - I, 110]

[5.19] It is the divine quality of mercy that enables the world to endure. The world's own merit is simply insufficient to sustain its existence:

> The heavenly quality of justice (*middat ha-din*) is rigorous (*qashah*), but the earthly quality of justice is lenient (*rafah*)... a quality which is gentle (*nohah*), dealing with the earth in compassion (*rahammim*). [CT: Gen. 9:12 - I, 65]

In other words, even the quality of justice had to be tempered with leniency in order to be applied on earth. Even earthly justice is not totally natural, then, in Nahmanides' sense of nature as a state of equilibrium where rewards and punishments are exactly commensurate with our acts, as effects are with their causes.

[5.20] Nahmanides argues that Moses' inquiry about God's Name at the Burning Bush was in fact an attempt to probe the depth of God's commitment to the Exodus. For Moses knew that a promise stemming from mercy would be more enduring than one stemming from justice, since mercy is freer than justice and truly effective, where justice is more reactive:

> In my view, Moses, who at the time was a great father in wisdom, at the very height of prophecy, by his question was asking... with which attribute (*be-'eizo middah*) he was to be sent to the Israelites... who would ask him if his mission was through the attribute of power (*El Shaddai*) which stood by the patriarchs, or the higher attribute of mercy, whereby the signs and wonders, formed *de novo*, were performed... For he knew that the Torah would not be given through the attribute of power, mentioned in connection with the patriarchs, but only by the Great Name whereby the world came into being. [CT: Exod. 3:13 - I, 290-291]

Nahmanides reasons that God appeared to Moses in his unique attribute of mercy, but to the patriarchs by the "weak" attribute of justice (CT: Exod. 6:21 - I, 303). For they were vouchsafed a mediated revelation over and above the knowledge one could glean from observation of nature's strict justice. They lacked the immediate revelation Moses received. Building on the view of Rashi, Nahmanides identifies God's unique Name as "the true attribute" (*middah amittit*) of mercy: Acting through mercy, God reveals himself as more than the Judge enforcing the equilibrium of the cosmos; he reveals his true character directly.

Chapter 6

The Land of Israel

[6.1] The centrality of the Land of Israel in the divine scheme of the universe is a momentous motif in Nahmanides' theology. The Land is the place on earth where the mediation of nature is least significant and the presence of hidden miracles most significant. Since keeping the commandments merits the experience of hidden miracles, even those commandments which are not contingent on dwelling in the Land assume a more intense meaning when practiced there. And the Land unites the strengths of hidden and public miracles. For, like the hidden miracles, divine providence there is continual; and, like the public miracles, providence there is frequently manifest. Of the blessings of the Land, Nahmanides writes:

> All these blessings are miracles. It is not simply by nature that the rains come [in due season].... Even though these are secret miracles in that the world proceeds in its accustomed manner (*ke-minhago*), they are made manifest (*mitparsim*) by the fact that they are continual throughout the Land of Israel... in a way unparallelled in all the world. It will be plain to all that this comes from the Lord. [CT: Lev. 26:11 - II, 185]

[6.2] The Sanctuary in Jerusalem epitomizes the special character of the Land:

> The mystery of the Sanctuary is that the glory which rested on Mount Sinai abides on it unseen (*be-nistar*). [CT: Exod. 25:1 - I, 453]

[6.3] Thus certain phenomena can occur only in the Land of Israel:

> This [disease, *tsara'at*] is not natural and does not occur [just anywhere] in the world... when Israel is wholly committed (*shelemim*) to the Lord, the spirit of the Lord will always be upon them to preserve their bodies, clothing, and houses in a good appearance... This will happen only in the chosen land... the matter is miraculous (*nes*). [CT: Lev. 13:47 - II, 75]

The word *tsara'at*, which designates the disease Nahmanides is discussing, is usually translated "leprosy," in accordance with LXX at Lev. 13:1 ff. (*lepras*). But unlike the disease long known as leprosy (now called Hansen's Disease), *tsara'at* afflicts clothing and houses as well as bodies. Further, its symptoms in human cases are more like those of eczema or psoriasis than like those of a dismembering disease like leprosy. Maimonides (*Hilkhot Tum'at Tsara'at*, 16.10) regards the term as generic, covering several different physical conditions. He designates *tsara'at* as supernatural (*'ot ve-pele*) and does not present any physical etiology for it. Instead he elaborates on the moral etiology suggested by the Rabbis (e.g., *Sifra*: Metsora, ed. Weiss, 73a re Deut. 24:9): *tsara'at* is a punishment for improper speech.

Halevi attributed the singular Jewish propensity for *tsara'at* to the unique physical characteristics of Jews and their possessions, resulting from the *Shekhinah* in Israel (*Kuzari*, 2.61-62). For him the etiology of the affliction was the subject of an "abstruse science" (*hokhmah mufla'ah* - 2.58, tr. Hirschfeld, 119). Nahmanides extends this approach to include the unique physical characteristics of the Land of Israel (cf. *Kuzari*, 2.15 ff.).

[6.4] The Land of Israel provides the optimal environment for keeping all of the commandments, even those which are also to be kept elsewhere:

> The forbidden sexual unions are matters of personal, bodily obligation (*hovat ha-guf*) and are not contingent on living in the Land of Israel. Yet this obligation has a mystical meaning... The Land of Israel is the center of of the inhabited world (*ha-yishuv*). It is the portion of the Lord, specially his. He did not give it over to any of his angels to govern, manage, or rule... For the root of all the commandments is addressed to those who dwell in the Land of Israel. [CT: Lev. 18:25 - II, 109]

[6.5] The theme is further developed in Nahmanides' discussion of the verse the Rabbis took as the Scriptural basis of the commandment to recite grace after meals (*birkat ha-mazon*): "You shall eat and be satisfied and bless the Lord your God upon the good land which he has given you" (Deut. 8:10):

> Our Rabbis have a tradition (*qibblu*) that this is a positive commandment [not just a promise of future prosperity and contentment]. The verse's sense (*ta'amo*) is that you ought to bless the Lord your God... And the sense (*ve-ta'am*) of 'upon the good land' is as if to say, '*and* do it there, *on* the good land.' He commands us to bless him whenever we are satisfied; *and* to do so on the land he has given us, which he shall cause us to inherit forever, and to find satisfaction in its goodness – although, of course, this obligation (*hiyyuv ha-mitsvah ha-zo't*) applies everywhere. [CT: Deut. 8:10 - II, 382]

Because the commandment to recite grace after meals, at all times everywhere, is derived from the verse by the Rabbis (B. Berakhot 20b-21a), Nahmanides calls this aspect of the verse "the obligation, (or obligatory force) of this commandment." An obligation (*hiyyuv*) is a commandment not dependent on conditions that can be avoided (see Maimonides, *Hilkhot Berakhot*, 11.2 based on B. Sotah 44b). If the obligation applies everywhere, Nahmanides asks, why is the commandment that states it linked to a phrase about the Land of Israel? To be sure, the commandment has broader application. Indeed, thanking God for food is seen as pertaining to non-Jews as well as Jews (Bereshit Rabbah 43.7 on Gen. 14:19; cf. Y.Berakhot 6.1/9d re Psalms 24:1.). But Nahmanides finds that even though the commandment is to be observed everywhere, one best appreciates the food God brings forth from the earth (*min ha'arets*, see B. Berakhot 38a-b) in that land (*ha'arets*, specifically the Land of Israel) where providence is most direct (see Y. Berakhot 6.1/10a re Psalms 72:16; B. Ketubot 111b; Bereshit Rabbah 15.7).

[6.6] The Land of Israel is the proximate locus of the manifestation of the *Shekhinah*. After giving the outward meaning of the verse, "Justice, justice shall you pursue" (Deut. 16:20) as an expression of the importance of zeal in human administration of the divine laws governing human affairs, Nahmanides offers a mystical interpretation based on his primary kabbalistic text, *Sefer ha-Bahir* (sec. 74-75). The interpretation connects the command to pursue justice with the remainder of the verse: "that you may live and inherit the land which the Lord your God gives you":

> The first "justice," which is literal justice (*tsedeq mamash*), is the *Shekhinah*... But what is the second "justice" that terrifies the righteous?... This is the higher justice (*tsedeq 'elyon*), through which you will live in the world-to-come. It is the great light stored up (*tsafun*) for the righteous in the hereafter (*le-'atid la-vo*). "And you shall inherit the land [that is, the world-to--come]," through the first "justice," which is the Land of Israel. [CT: Deut. 16:20 - II, 419]

This comment plays on the double meaning of 'the land' in rabbinic thought, where it means either the Land of Israel (e.g., Hullin 16b re Deut. 12:20) or the world-to-come (e.g., M. Sanhedrin 10.1 re Isaiah 60:21). The kabbalistic gloss connects the two seemingly separate meanings of the word.

[6.7] The sanctity of the Land of Israel results from its centrality, marked for Nahmanides by the site of the archetypal heavenly Temple:

> From antiquity the nations knew that this place [Jerusalem] is the choicest site, the center of the inhabited world (*ha-yishuv*). Perhaps they knew from some tradition that its excellence (*ma'alato*) is because it directly faces the heavenly Temple where God's Presence (*Shekhinato*) is called "Justice" (*tsedeq*). [CT: Gen. 14:18 - I, 86-87]

[6.8] The Land of Israel is the only remnant of the earth as it was before human sin became manifest. It is wholly under direct providence, without the mediation of nature:

> When the commandments are fulfilled there, the Land of Israel will be as the world was at its beginning, before the the first man's sin... When Scripture says "and it was so" [Gen. 1:30], this refers to the nature which was placed in creatures forever... The animals of the Land of Israel will be in a state of perfection, their vicious behavior (*ra'at minhagam*) will cease, and they will revert to the primordial nature (*ha-teva ha-ri'shon*) impressed on them at the time of their creation... Thus Scripture states that in the days of the redeemer, who will come out of the stock of Jesse, peace will return to the world and carnage (*ha-teref*) will cease [Isaiah 11:1-9]. The nature of the animals will be once again as it was at the beginning. [CT: Lev. 26:6 - II, 183]

[6.9] The Land of Israel not only is the place least subject to the mediation of nature, it is in a way itself an intermediary of God's governance:

> God does not attend to anything, as it were (*kivyakhol*), but it; and it is through this attention that he attends to all other lands... there is in this a deep mystery, inasmuch as this land is attended to in every way. It is all things, and all other lands in truth are nurtured from it. [CT: Deut. 11:10 - II, 393]

[6.10] The sanctity of the Land of Israel stems from the fact that it is the earthly place where the connection with the transcendent reality of the world-to-come is most proximate. It is the location of the Garden of Eden:

> He figured in this portentous place [the Garden of Eden] all the work of the upper world. It is the world of souls given in material form, so that one can understand through it the constitution of every creature: bodily, spiritual (*nafshi*), and angelic... It is the most estimable place in the lower world (*'olam ha-shafal*). For it is the center of the world, leading directly to the upper world. So the divine will be seen there more frequently than anywhere else on earth. We believe that the Land of Israel and Jerusalem are the most important places, especially suited for prophecy because of this direct connection [with the upper world], and especially with the [heavenly] Temple, which is the throne of the Lord. [KR: *Torat ha-Adam*: Sha'ar ha-Gemul - II, 296]

[6.11] Nahmanides draws on the ancient idea that all the nations of the world are under the control of angelic intermediaries, whereas Israel is under the direct control of God himself (LXX at Deut. 32:8; Siracides 17:17; B. Shabbat 156a). But he stresses the centrality of the Land of Israel at least as much as that of the people of Israel:

> Why is it called "the land of the Lord" (Hos. 9:3)? Is not the whole world the land of the Lord? He created everything, and all is his. The basis of an answer is found in the verse: "when the Most High gave the nations their portions, differentiating the human race (*benei adam*), he set the boundaries according to the numbers of the children of Israel. For the portion of the Lord is his people, etc." (Deut. 32:8-9). The meaning is that the Lord created heaven and earth and imparted power over the lower beings to the higher beings, causing a particular star or constellation to rule over each people in its land, as is known from the science of astrology (*be-hokhmat ha-itstagninut*)... The Lord, glorious is he, is the supreme God and lord of the entire world. But the Land of Israel is the center of the habitable world (*emtza'ut ha-yishuv*), the Lord's own special portion. He did not place any angel over it as a magistrate, administrator or governor... Outside the Land of Israel, even though everything is for the sake of his Glorious Name, there is no perfect purity, because of the ministering angels who govern there, and peoples go astray after their officials, even worshipping them... This is the meaning of the rabbinic statement (T. 'Avodah Zarah 4.5; B.Ketubot 110b), "whoever dwells outside the Land of Israel is like one who has no God." [KR: *Sermon for Rosh Hashanah* - I, 249-50]

[6.12] Just as the nations of the world are not under direct providence but are related to God through intermediate heavenly powers, so are all other lands related to God. Only the Land of Israel is directly ruled by God:

> The most honored Lord created everything and placed earthly beings (*tahtonim*) in the power of higher beings (*'elyonim*), giving them power over every people in its land, to each a definite star and constellation, which "the Lord your God apportioned (*halaq*)" (Deut. 4:19)... The constellations are in heaven, and above them are the higher angels, who rule over them... That is why we say God is "king of kings." [KR: *Sermon on Kohelet* - I, 200-01]

[6.13] The connection between the commandments of the Torah and the Land of Israel colors Nahmanides' discussion of an opinion held by many of the Rabbis that the patriarchs observed the entire Torah before it was revealed at Mount Sinai (M. Kidd. 4.14/ end; B. Yoma 28b; Y. Berakhot 2.3/4c; Bereshit Rabbah 95.3; Louis Ginzberg, *Legends of the Jews* [Philadelphia: Jewish Publication Society of America, 1925] **5**.259, n. 275). Nahmanides seems more inclined to the opposing view, that the patriarchs kept only the Noahide Commandments and circumcision, and that no one kept the entire Torah until it was revealed at Sinai (B. Sanhedrin 56b; Shir ha-Shirim Rabbah 1.16; Maimonides, *Hilkhot Melakhim*, 9.1; KR: *Torat ha-Shem Temimah* - I, 173). But in commenting on Gen. 26:5 (CT - I, 151) he argues that if the maximal opinion is correct (*ve'im ken*, CT - I, 149) the patriarchal observance was only in the Land of Israel. The logic is that if the commandments can be observed fully by the people of Israel only in the Land of Israel, then single individuals, without the support of the community, would surely require the Land to be able to observe the full complement of the commandments.

> Abraham our father learned the whole Torah through the holy spirit... and observed it as one who was not actually commanded to do so, but kept it voluntarily. Yet his observance was only in the Land of Israel. [CT: Gen. 26:5 - I, 150]

The idea that one may observe what has not been commanded, with a lesser reward than for obeying explicit commands (B. Kiddushin 31a; Tos., s.v. *gadol*; *Hiddushei ha-Ramban ad loc.*, p. 296), allows Nahmanides to open a middle ground between the maximalist and minimalist views of patriarchal observance. In a different way, the Rabbis too saw the Land of Israel as the optimal locale for observing the *mitsvot* (*Sifre*: Devarim, no. 43 re Deut. 11:17-18, ed. Finkelstein, 102. – I thank David Berger for this reference.)

[6.14] For reasons clearly linked to his historical situation, Nahmanides saw in the Torah a positive obligation for every Jew at all times to live in the Land of Israel:

> In my view, to live in the Land of Israel is a positive commandment... and what I have explained is the essence of the matter. [CT: Num. 33:53 - II, 335]

[6.15] Nahmanides diagrees here with Rashi, whose *Commentary on the Torah* understands the words, "and you shall dwell therein" (Num. 33:53) as an assurance of reward: *If* during the Israelite conquest of Canaan, you properly dispossess the Canaanites, *then* you shall dwell in safety in the land. Nahmanides is especially critical of Maimonides for not listing the *mitsvah* of dwelling in the Land of Israel as one of the 613 commandments of the Written Torah. He does not consider it sufficient that neither Rashi nor Maimonides disputed the merit of dwelling in the Land:

> The fourth *mitsvah* we are given is to inherit the Land which the Lord, exalted be he, gave our fathers... not abandon it to other nations or to desolation... We are commanded to inherit the Land and dwell in it. This is a positive commandment for all generations, for each of us, even in time of exile, as is known from numerous passages in the Talmud. [*Notes on Maimonides' Sefer ha-Mitsvot*: Addenda, pos. no. 4, pp. 244-46]

[6.16] The sanctity of the Land of Israel is such that it is sinful to abandon it, even through economic hardship. Of Abraham's descent into Egypt after reaching the Land at God's behest, Nahmanides writes:

> Know also... that his departure from the Land because of the famine was an advertant sin (*'avon*). For God would have saved him from death. It was on account of this deed that it was decreed that his descendents would be exiled in the land of Egypt under Pharaoh's rule. [CT: Gen. 12:9 - I, 79-80]

Nahmanides identifies two sins in the text: first, Abraham's passing off his wife as his sister, risking her being taken into Pharaoh's harem and violated. But that sin was inadvertant (*bi-shegagah*). The second, his descent into Egypt, was advertant. (For the distinction, M. Yoma 4.2; Maimonides, *Commentary on the Mishnah ad loc.*) The commentators on Nahmanides' *Commentary on the Torah* have trouble explaining why one sin was advertant, and the other inadvertant and so less serious (Chavel, note on CT - I, 79). But perhaps we can connect Nahmanides' greater concern over desertion of the Land with a fear lest that lapse be repeated in later generations, an event more likely than the temptation to pass off one's wife as a sister.

[6.17] The Land of Israel is not only the perfect environment for fulfilling the commandments, but it has the power to alter some of our obligations. Thus in commenting on a verse which seems to call for unreserved use and enjoyment of the Land by the conquering Israelites, Nahmanides elaborates on a Talmudic gloss:

> The goods to be found in the full houses are permitted, even if they contain things forbidden by the Torah [Hullin 17a]... and even when lives are not at risk. [CT: Deut. 6:10 - II, 373]

Maimonides (*Hilkhot Melakhim*, 8.1) had derived the Talmudic permission from a concern that in wartime soldiers might be on the verge of starvation. He sees the ruling as a dispensation based on the commandment to preserve life even at the cost of violating a negative precept (B. Sanhedrin 74a re Lev. 18:5; B. Yoma 85b). But Nahmanides, noting that the Talmudic permission applies even when there is no danger, argues that the Land, at least in some cases, by its very sanctity, changes the commandments altogether. (But cf. Semahot 7.8; B. Kiddushin 21b-22a; B. Sanhedrin 59a for the application of wartime dispensations in non-life-threatening situations not confined to the Land of Israel; see *Sifre*: Devarim, no. 211 re Deut. 21:10, ed. Finkelstein, 245).

[6.18] Nahmanides never misses an opportunity to show how the sanctity of the Land of Israel anchors the specifics of many of the commandments, both Scriptural and rabbinic. An early example is seen in his explanation of the ruling (M. Megillah 1.1) that the book of Esther must be read on the fifteenth of Adar in cities walled since the time of Joshua, but on the fourteenth in all other cities and towns. Marvelling that the Rabbis would so sharply differentiate Jewish practices in two kinds of place, Nahmanides introduces the sanctity of the Land of Israel as the explanation:

> When I examined the Scriptural texts, the problem was settled for me. Clearly at the time of the miracle the Jewish people had already received the order to go back up to the Land with Cyrus' permission and had resettled in their cities... When Ahasuerus commanded that the Jews be killed and massacred, the open towns and unwalled cities were in the gravest peril. There was greater danger that they would be overrun by the enemy than there was for walled cities... So the miracle was greater there... And the reason for the decree [by Mordecai and Esther – Esther 9:20-21] differentiating two separate days for celebration of the miracle is that open towns in the days of Ahasuerus took precedence over walled cities. For the root of the miracle was for those Jews in the Land of Israel, which was desolate and still had not been rebuilt... Yet

> it was not right that Jerusalem, the holy city, and the rest of the ruined cities of Judah and Israel should be classed with open towns. So the ranking of a city was based on its condition at the time of Joshua... This is because they treated the Land of Israel with honor. [*Hiddushei ha-Ramban ha-Shalem*: B. Megillah 2a, pp. 6-7]

Nahmanides here follows R. Seemon in the Palestinian Talmud (Y. Megillah 1.1/70a), where it becomes clear that the cities in the Land of Israel, which were unwalled at the time of Mordecai and Esther, should not be considered less important than the foreign capital of Shushan, which was walled at that time. Nahmanides' argues that attention should be paid to the Land of Israel on two counts: (1) the greater miracle took place there because of the Land's greater vulnerability, since it had only unwalled cities at the time; (2) the cities of the Land of Israel should not be put in a less honorable category than the foreign capital of Shushan.

[6.19] Nahmanides does not make the sanctity of the Land of Israel independent of the relation of the Land to the people of Israel. The Land is sanctified and blessed because it is included in the perpetual covenant between God and Israel. Thus, in commenting on the verse, "And I shall remember My covenant with Jacob, and my covenant with Isaac, and my covenant with Abraham shall I remember, and the Land shall I remember" (Lev. 26:42), Nahmanides writes:

> In truth (*'al derekh ha-'emet*) it should be said that God remembered Jacob and Isaac and Abraham, who are parties to a covenant (*benei berit*). For all of the qualities ascribed to them are so when they are so covenanted. But since the Land of Israel is included along with them, God will remember it too in that totality (*bi-khlal*). Our Rabbis hinted at this when they said (Vayiqra Rabbah 36.7), "Why did He privilege (*zekhut*) the Land along with them? R. Simeon ben Laqish said that it is like a lord who had three daughters raised by a maidservant. Whenever the lord asked after the welfare of his daughters, he would also say, "Inquire for me too about the welfare of the one who is raising them." [CT: Lev. 26:42 - II, 191]

Chapter 7

The Commandments

[7.1] Our relationship with God is founded in faith. Faith (*emunah*) is not just a state of consciousness; it entails practice. All the commandments of the Torah are acts of faith. Their proper performance must recognize God as he is and acknowledge him as who he is, the God who revealed himself to Israel in the public miracles (*nissim mefursamim*). Since what we know about God comes from history, the locus of faith is memory (*Notes on Maimonides' Sefer ha-Mitsvot*, pos. no. 1, p. 261). Faith is fulfilled when the memory of God's mighty acts is expressed in the commandments that commemorate those acts as Israel experienced them:

> He commanded us to have faith in the unique God, exalted be he: that he exists, that he is the One who understands and can do all things. Our faith should be unified in intending (*ve-she-niyyahed*) these atttributes, for all honor is his. So he commanded us to honor the mention of his Name, to make a perpetual sign and remembrance (*siman ve-zikaron tamid*) to let us know that God created everything. [CT: Exod. 20:8 - I, 398]

[7.2] Acceptance of the commandments depends on acceptance of God's reality and particular providence:

> We must believe that God knows individual persons (*'ishim*) in all their particularities, both heavenly (*ha-'elyonim*) and earthly persons (*ve-ha-tahtonim*), their deeds and thoughts, past, present and future. For he is their maker, the bestower of the existence they now have, their creator out of absolute nothingness (*me-'afeisah muhletet*)... From this we move to faith in God's providence (*ha-hashgahah*)... whence we can affirm

> (*titkayyem*) the true authority of the Torah and the commandments. For inasmuch as we believe that God knows and cares for us, our faith extends to prophecy, and we believe that God, exalted be he, knows and cares, commands and admonishes, that is, commands us to do what is good and right and reproves us about what is evil. He protects us and preserves for us all the good consequences mentioned in the Torah, and will bring upon trangressors the retribution he decreed for them. [KR: *Commentary on Job*, intro. - I, 17-18]

For Nahmanides, "affirmation" (*qiyyum*) of the authority of the Torah and the commandments is an act of faith, prior to the performance of any of the individual commandments (CT: Deut. 27:26 - II, 472; *supra*, 2.24). It is the cognitive side of *kavvanah*. Emotively, one must direct the heart to God. Cognitively, one is to know as much as humanly possible about the God to whom one's heart is so directed (CT: Exod. 15:2 - I, 354-55 re *Mekhilta*: Be-shalah, ed. Horovitz-Rabin, 128). Both the cognitive and emotive sides of faith are required in the proper observance of the commandments.

[7.3] Since all the commandments have reasons, each with a unique function in the divine economy of the cosmos, one is obligated to discern the reason for each commandment and make it the intention (*kavvanah*) of one's observance. Even in areas of life that are left to private discretion (*reshut*), one must find the proper intention toward the divine:

> Indeed, one can be a wretch (*naval*) while conforming to the behavior the the Torah permits (*bi-reshut ha-Torah*). Thus, having specified the acts it absolutely prohibits, Scripture commanded in more general terms that one should keep his distance even from what is permitted. [CT: Lev. 19:1 - II, 15]

Nahmanides means that one should shun excess and vulgarity even in permitted eating, drinking and sexual expression. For physical pleasure is not the *summum bonum*. Nahmanides favors the Talmudic opinion that the Nazirite is a saint, as opposed to the alternative Talmudic view that such an ascetic is a sinner for denying himself pleasures the Torah normally permits (B. Ta'anit 10a and parallels; for the critique of asceticism, see Y. Berakhot 2.9 / 5d; Y. Nedarim 9.1 / 41b; B. Baba Batra 60b; and especially Maimonides, *Shemonah Peraqim*, chap.4, ed. Kafih (Jerusalem: Mosad Harav Kook, 1965), 254 [cf. *Moreh*, 3.48]). For Maimonides, holiness is ultimately active partnership with God, which grows from recognition of God's creative governance of the world (*Moreh*, 3.54, end). What is required for this, as for all piety, is not asceticism but reasonable restraint of excess (*Hilkhot De'ot*, 1.4-6). For Nahmanides, however, extra self-restraint, for the sake of God, can itself be a holy act. Asceticism characterized much of Jewish mysticism, whether Spanish Kabbalah or German *Hasidut* (see Scholem, *Origins of the Kabbalah*, 229 ff.) The trend goes back to the times of the Geonim and *Hekhalot* mysticism (see Scholem, *Major Trends in Jewish Mysticism*, 49-50). Even though such asceticism long predates Nahmanides, his endorsement gave it the added authority of his stature as a halakhist.

[7.4] Nahmanides regards the Nazarite's return to the ordinary world as a sinful descent from a higher spiritual plane:

> The reason for the sin-offering (*hat'at*) the Nazirite offers on the day of the completion of his Nazirite vow has not been explicated. According to the plain meaning... it is right that he should be a Nazirite and be sanctified to God... Indeed, he needs atonement for returning to the impurity of the pleasures of the world. [CT: Num. 6:11 - II, 215]

[7.5] Nahmanides cannot say that every commandment must be performed with the proper intention in order to be legally valid, but he does indicate that the full realization of the commandments requires proper intention:

> It is known that whoever performs a commandment but does not understand it has not fulfilled it completely (*bi--shlemut*)... For you are obligated to remember the great miracle performed for you. [KR: *Torat ha-Shem Temimah* - I, 151]

To act without awareness of the act's intent is to fall short of the very requirement of the commandment itself. For Nahmanides, intention here does not mean abstract contemplation of the Godhead but concentration on the specific miracle the act commemorates.

[7.6] The level of intention (*kavvanah*) one must have in order to fulfill a commandment is the subject of a long, inconclusive debate in the Talmud (B. Rosh Hashanah 28a *et seq.*). For Nahmanides intention is critical in allowing us to acknowledge God's will as the source of a commandment and God's wisdom in the specification of its purpose. Through intention one, as it were, follows the purpose of God. Admitting that there are many opinions on the subject of *kavvanah*, Nahmanides grounds a maximalist argument on a passage in the Mishnah: "If one were reading in the Torah [Deut. 6:4-9, the textual content of the *Shema*] and the time for the liturgical recitation of the *Shema* arrived, if one's heart intended this specific commandment, he has fulfilled it; if not, he has not" [M. Berakhot 2.1].

> Regarding the matter of intention in blowing the shofar: if one blew it only to make a musical sound, the issue is debated in the Talmud and among the Geonim... Rabbenu Hai wrote

> that even though it is the law that if one performs a commandment without the intention he has still fulfilled it, nevertheless, let one regularly have intent when performing the commandments. In all humility, we have a proof for the view of the author of *Halakhot Gedolot* [who accepts the maximalist view at the end of his treatement of the laws of Rosh Hashanah] from the law at the beginning of the second chapter of the Mishnah, Berakhot [about the *Shema*]. [KR: *Sermon for Rosh Hashanah* - I, 241]

Nahmanides confesses that he cannot presume to have settled the practical debate among the Geonim, but theologically he certainly has settled the matter. Those influenced by the kabbalistic tradition, of which Nahmanides was such a key source, emphasized the necessity of *kavvanah*, not only on general theological grounds, but on specific halakhic grounds as well, whenever possible (see, especially, Joseph Karo, *Shulhan 'Arukh*: 'Orah Hayyim, 60.4; also, R. J. Z. Werblowsky, *Joseph Karo: Lawyer and Mystic* [Philadelphia: JPS, 1977], 162-63).

[7.7] In the significance he assigns to *kavvanah*, Nahmanides disagrees with Maimonides about the verse, "to serve Him with all your heart" (Deut. 11:13). Maimonides interprets the rabbinic comment on this verse, "this is prayer... the service of the heart" (*Sifre*: Devarim, no. 41, ed. Finkelstein, 87-88; B. Ta'anit 2a) as finding there a literal mandate for prayer (*Sefer ha-Mitzvot*, pos. no. 5), although the actual content of formal worship is formulated by the Rabbis (*Hilkhot Tefillah*,1.1). Nahmanides sees the verse as referring to all the commandments of the Torah. For him the allusion to prayer is a homiletical inference (*'asmakhta*):

> The essential meaning of the verse "to serve him with all your heart" (Deut. 11:13) is that it is a positive commandment that all our works be for God, exalted be he, be done with all our heart. That means with proper and full intention, for God's sake and without any evil thought. We should not perform the commandments without intention or doubting that they have any benefit (*to'elet*). [*Notes to Maimonides' Sefer ha-Mitzvot*, pos. no. 5, p. 156]

[7.8] So central is intention that fulfillment of a commandment for the wrong reason can be a sin. Thus the Egyptian enslavement of the Israelites was part of the divine plan, but sinful, nonetheless:

> So when God decreed Israel's servitude in Egypt, they arose and forcibly enslaved them... When the decree goes forth by a prophet... there is merit in performing it... but if one heard

> the commandment [to kill] and then killed in hatred or for the sake of plunder, he is to be punished, since his intent is sinful. For the Egyptians knew that it was a commandment of the Lord [that Israel be enslaved by them]. [CT: Gen. 15:14 - I, 94]

[7.9] Because the foundation of the Torah, which is God's sovereignty over the universe, is known through historical experience, affirmation of that experience has priority even over the study of the Torah's precepts. The historical experience par excellence is the theophany at Sinai. Thus the Rabbis gloss the verse, "Be very careful and take great care with your own life lest you forget the things your eyes saw... all the days of your life, and you shall make them known to your children and your children's children" (Deut. 4:9) as intending the duty to educate one's progeny in the Torah's precepts (B. Kiddushin 30a). But Nahmanides treats this gloss as homiletical (*asmakhta*). He finds the literal commandment at a much deeper level:

> The second commandment is that we not forget the theophany at Mount Sinai... for it is a major principle (*yesod gadol*) of the Torah... Do not make the mistake of interpreting this verse as a mere homily about teaching the Torah to one's grandchildren. For faith in the Torah itself (*emunat ha-Torah*) is what is meant here by study of the Torah... *This* is what is to be transmitted from generation to generation. [*Notes on Maimonides' Sefer ha-Mitzvot*: Addenda, neg. no. 2, p. 396]

God's existence, power, and will were revealed to Israel at Sinai: "They are the ones who know and are the witnesses (*'edim*) to all these things" (CT: Exod. 20:2 - I, 388). Israel's witness is historical. A witness is one who was present at an event and reports it to the community. Events require witnesses because they are singular. Those not actually present must learn from the accounts of those whom they can trust. With ordinary processes of nature, special witnesses are not required. For these are accessible to all. No one need learn of them from a story told by someone else. Scientific demonstration assumes that what it reports is, at least in principle, accessible to any observer. For the principles it demonstrates are always present, even if the phenomena that manifest them are not.

The difference between historical witness and scientific demonstration is exemplified in the rabbinic discussion of the institution of determining the exact time of the New Moon, the key point of reference in regulating the Jewish calendar. (For the historic background, see M. M. Kasher, *Torah Shlemah* [New York: n.p., 1949] XIII). For the Rabbis, the requirement of eyewitnesses to the appearance of the New Moon (M. Rosh Hashanah 1.6 *et seq.*) is not a *sine qua non* for calendrical purposes (B. Betsah 4b). Witnesses are preferred when the Sanhedrin is actually functioning in the Land of Israel. But otherwise the calculations made by the Rabbis in

Talmudic times fix the Jewish calendar (see *Notes on Maimonides' Sefer ha-Mitsvot*, pos. no. 153, p. 214 and Maimonides' text on pp. 211-12): The matter is essentially one of scientific demonstration (Maimonides, *Hilkhot Qiddush ha-Hodesh*, 1.6; 5.2-3; 11.1-4; 17.24), not a singular experience. In the historical context witnesses *affirm* what needs to be known by others; in the scientific context witnesses merely *confirm* what others can in principle know for themselves.

In treating the role of witness in revelation, Nahmanides follows Judah Halevi, for whom Judaism rests ultimately on the Sinai theophany and the testimony of the entire people of Israel, who experienced it (*Kuzari*, 1.48). God's presence is manifest in unique historical events. For Maimonides, by contrast, the content of the Sinai theophany itself is credible because the first two commandments of the decalogue are rationally evident truths grounding all the other commandments–the positive ones on the basis of "I am the Lord your God"; the negative, on the basis of "there shall be no other gods" (*Moreh Nevukhim*, 2.33; *Sefer ha-Mitsvot*, pos. no. 1, neg. no. 1; *Hilkhot Yesodei ha-Torah*, 1.6; cf. the Talmudic source for this opinion, B. Makkot 24a, where the foundation of these two commandments in revelation is the primary emphasis). For Maimonides it is rational certitude that clears the Sinai experience of the charge that it might have been a mass delusion (*Hilkhot Yesodei ha-Torah*, 8.1-3). God's reality is known through reason's apprehension of nature. So historical witness has the secondary role that witnesses play in ascertaining the New Moon. Further, Maimonides argues, testimony is not itself rationally demonstrable. It is only more or less credible. Thus Maimonides designates the whole juridical institution of witness (*'edut*) as one that we are commanded to accept, despite the indemonstrability of what is witnessed and the constant possibility of deception or delusion (*Hilkhot Yesodei ha-Torah*, 7.7; *Hilkhot 'Edut*, 18.3; *Hilkhot Sanhedrin*, 18.6). For Halvei and Nahmanides the event of revelation is the foundation of its content. For Maimonides, the event of revelation is the occasion in which what has always been true in principle (*ratio per se*) is discovered by us (*ratio quoad nos*).

[7.10] For Nahmanides, human experience of the world is on three basic levels: 1) ordinary experience of the familiar natural order; 2) public miracles, where God's power upsets the ordinary state of nature, so as to jolt those who experience these great events into a higher awareness of God's workings in the world; and 3) secret miracles, mainifesting the constant providence of God. Human action, as structured by the Torah in its commandments, is correlated with these three levels of experience; they are interrelated, in that one commandment may have several reasons.

> The commandments of the Lord each have many reasons. For each has many benefits (*to'elet*), both for the body and for the soul. [CT: Exod. 20:23 - I, 411]

[7.11] Although Nahmanides accepts multiple reasons for each commandment, he rejects rationales that he considers specious:

> Maimonides' rationale for the sacrifices [*Moreh*, 3.46]... is empty speculation (*divrei hav'ai*)... It is better to heed the reason of those who say that it is because the deeds of a human being are constituted by thought, speech, and action, so God commanded that when someone sins, he is to bring a sacrifice and press his hands on it, to signify the act (*ke-neged ha--ma'aseh*), confess with his mouth, to signify the word, and burn the entrails and kidneys, which are the organs of thought and desire... These words are readily accessible and draw the heart like the words of *Aggadah* [see B. Shabbat 87a; B. Baba Batra 10a re Prov. 3:35]. But in terms of higher truth (*'al derekh ha-'emet*), there is a hidden mystery (*sod ne'elam*) in the sacrifices. [CT: Lev. 1:9 - II, 11-12]

The view of Maimonides that Nahmanides criticizes here is that the sacrifices were necessary historically, as a form of worship to which the people of Israel were accustomed. They were a compromise with cultural reality, but carefully purged of any idolatrous associations. Nahmanides objects that sacrificial worship is much too central in Judaism for so historically contingent a rationale to be true. A second line of interpretation (whose author he does not name, although it resembles an approach suggested in Ibn Ezra's *Commentary on the Torah*: Lev. 1:4 following Vayiqra Rabbah 7.3) would be preferable: that the sacrifices symbolize true contrition and a spirit of self-sacrifice in coming before God. The same point is later emphasized by the *Zohar* (Vayiqra, 3:9b and by Bahya ben Asher's *Commentary on the Torah* on this same verse.) But Nahmanides finds the deepest meaning of the sacrifices in a divine reality. In essence, he holds, they fulfill divine needs. This is the view of Kabbalah, and Nahmanides' approach here deeply influenced later kabbalists (see I. Tishby, *Mishnat ha-Zohar*, **2**.194 ff.)

[7.12] Despite Nahmanides' rejection of Maimonides' general rationale for the sacrificial system, he agrees that Maimonides was right in interpreting certain cultic prohibitions as anti-idolatrous in intent:

> It is plausible (*yitakhen*) to interpret the prohibitions of leaven and honey on the altar as Maimonides does in the *Moreh Nevukhim* [3.46], when he says that he found in the books of the ancient idolators that it was their custom, in practicing pagan worship, to offer their meal offerings in leavened form and to mingle honey in all their sacrifices. [CT: Lev. 2:2 - II, 17-18]

[7.13] A theology which finds reasons for God's commandments cannot view them as mere positive decrees. Rather, they must be seen as warranted either by the benefits they afford in improving human relations, or by the good they bring to the relationship of God and man. This latter relationship, constituted by revelation, is immutable. But ultimately all the commandments constitute the relationship between God and man. So all are immmutable (CT: Exod. 15:26 - I, 361). They cannot be repealed by mere human authority. For the divine determination of what is good for humans always takes precedence over human notions. Human projections of what is good for humans are still essentially human, so they are subject to human repeal. Nahmanides stresses the distinction in a halakhic analysis of oaths:

> Some say that [the oath to accept the Torah at Mount Sinai] was made with divine consent (*'al da'at ha-Maqom*)... and that Moses' consent was not needed, except inasmuch as he was made the spokesman of the [human] court to their Father in heaven... There is one interpreter who says the correct Talmudic text reads, "by divine consent and that of his angelic entourage (*u-famaliah shelo*)," but that is erroneous... One interpreter says that the rule that communal oaths to God can be repealed does not apply to any commandment of God, for what is sworn according to God's will (*'al da'ato*) cannot be annulled (*hafarah*), since his commandments stand forever. For "God is not a man that he would lie" (Num. 23:19). But what the community vows in matters deemed optional (*bi-dvar reshut*), where they have connected their consent with that of God, can be repealed, and they can agree to permit its violation... and God concurs with their decision. To me it seems that the proper legal formula for such oaths should be: "By divine consent and that of the congregation (*kenesset*) of Israel with him"... That is, the consent of the many. Yet, what the community swears by invoking divine consent, that they may repeal (*yesh hetter*). For they have not prohibited themselves from changing it, inasmuch as they themselves initiated it. [*Hiddushei ha-Ramban ha-Shalem*: Shevu'ot 29b, pp. 112-13]
>
> When it says in the Talmud [B. Shevu'ot 29b] that "by the consent of God" means what cannot be repealed, the one who stated this assumed that this applies only to the oath involved in accepting the Torah. For God would not agree to void (*le-vattel*) even one letter of the Torah. But in an essentially optional matter, God would recognize the need to prohibit something now and later permit it. [*Hiddushei ha-Ramban ha-Shalem*: Mishpat ha-Herem, p. 287]

Thus, although Nahmanides sees rabbinic legislation as an expression of divine law (*Notes on Maimonides' Sefer ha-Mitsvot*, shoresh 1), he sees a difference between Scriptural and rabbinic law, in that rabbinic law may be repealed.

[7.14] For Nahmanides, then, God decrees in the Torah what he sees is needed by human beings. But he permits human authorities to make their own, mutable decrees in those areas not determined by the mandates of the Torah. God not only permits but specifically enjoins this activity, thus imparting divine authority to human laws:

> Further, 'by divine consent' is also attached to rabbinic commandments. For if one were to say that divine consent is mentioned only in the oath that Moses had Israel take... but is not attached to our oaths and condemnations (*ve-haramim*), then why did our ancestors mention divine consent in connection with [their] prohibitions — unless God was in accord? He, exalted be his name, concurs that we may do what is good and right in his eyes *and* in the eyes of human beings. [*Hiddushei ha-Ramban ha-Shalem*: Mishpat ha-Herem, p. 299]

[7.15] The specific commandments do not presuppose miracles either secret or public. Most presume the ordinary order of nature. A number of the commandments can be seen to serve ordinary human needs. Nahmanides, who is often thought to be an anti-rationalist, finds natural law in the Torah itself. He is quite open about this in a number of places, especially in his *Commentary on the Torah*. Concerning the punishment of the generation of the Flood, he writes:

> For punishment was not decreed against them except for violence (*hamas*). For this [the unacceptability of lawlessness] is a rational matter (*'inyan muskal*) which does not depend on revelation (*Torah*). [CT: Gen. 6:2 - I, 48]

[7.16] Following a trend evident in natural law theory since the time of the Stoic philosophers and Roman jurists, Nahmanides regards the prohibition of anarchic violence as recognized by public consensus and well known to reason:

> Violence is robbery and oppression... a sin which is known and publicly recognized (*mefursam*)... for it is a rational commandment (*mitsvah muskelet*), whose prohibition needs no prophetic commandment. [CT: Gen. 6:13 - I, 52]

[7.17] Regarding rational rules, Nahmanides sometimes finds a precedent in the moral standards of the ancients (CT: Gen. 19:32 -I, 119]. He even sees rational content in *mitsvot* not usually deemed rational commandments:

> For the ancient sages, before the giving of the Torah, knew that there is a great utility (*to'elet*) in levirate marriage. [CT: Gen. 29:27 - I, 215]

[7.18] The universally accepted natural law is the minimal requirement for Jews, supplemented greatly by the revealed law of the Torah:

> Thus you find that the patriarchs and the prophets conducted themselves in the universally accepted moral manner (*derekh erets*)... if the patriarchs and prophets who came to do God's will conducted themselves in a universally accepted moral way, how much more so should ordinary people. [CT: Exod. 12:21 - I, 334]

[7.19] Jewish revelation shares many general points with natural law and with Noahide law. Its advantage lies in its revealed particularities. Just as the superiority of human beings over animals is evidenced by the special providence they enjoy, so the particularities of revealed law show the superiority of Israel over the other nations:

> It is seen from this [the presentation of the Noahide laws in B. Sanhedrin 56b] that the Noahides were given their commandments in general (*bi-khelalut*) not specific terms... Thus the people had only general commandments until they came to Mount Sinai, where the commandments were spelled out for them in their particularities... Now all of these matters [civil and criminal laws] are grouped together in one overarching category, *mishpat*. [*Notes on Maimonides' Sefer ha-Mitzvot*, shoresh 14, p. 143]

The 15th century Spanish Jewish theologian, Joseph Albo made much the same point about the superiority of divine law over natural law and positive human law (*Sefer ha-'Iqqarim*, 1.8; cf. Thomas Aquinas, *Summa Theologiae*, 2-1, q. 99, a. 2). But he does not mention Nahmanides as a source for his view. In maintaining the ultimate superiority of a rich system of specific precepts over a body of moral generalitiies, Nahmanides was surely influenced by the opening of Judah Halevi's *Kuzari* (1, intro.), where the philosophically minded, king of the Khazars is is told in a dream that God approves of his general intentions but not of his specific actions. It is this criticism that launches the quest which brings the king ultimately to Judaism.

[7.20] Even though natural justice seems to be an essentially human reality, human beings are capable of justice only because of a unique telos, which is to be close to God. Hence, we are distinguished from the animals both theologically and morally. Glossing Elihu's remark in the Book of Job that God "teaches us more than the beasts of the earth and makes us wiser than the birds of the heavens" (Job 35:11), Nahmanides explains:

> Elihu says that God taught us to know him and to become wise about his deeds in ways that the animals are not. That is why he did not want us to harm one another, an instinct which he placed in animals, so that they tear each other apart... Elihu said this to explicate the reason for individual providence: Because we recognize our Creator and gain wisdom about his deeds, we are subject to his commandments. [KR: *Commentary on Job* 35:11 - I, 106-07]

The argument assumes that even before the giving of the Torah, there was a natural human recognition of elementary justice, based on recognition of the order of creation, which was recognized as the work of God.

[7.21] Nahmanides stresses that the commandments given shortly before the revelation of the Torah at Sinai are not Torah in the strict sense but a kind of moral preparation. They are not even distinctively Jewish:

> These were moral admonitions, lest they become like the camps of plunderers who shamelessly commit every kind of atrocity... These are not the statutes and ordinances of the Torah. They are civil regulations (*hanhagot ve-yishuv ha-medinot*) like the terms set by Joshua as recalled by the sages. [CT: Exod. 15:25 - I, 359]

Although the terms set by Joshua were clearly stipulated in connection with the entrance of the Israelites into the Land of Israel (B. Baba Kama 80b-81a), Maimonides says that they apply everywhere (*Hilkhot Nizqei Mamon*, 5.5). If so, their appeal must be to universal reasoning. Here Nahmanides follows the view of Maimonides.

[7.22] Again, like Maimonides, he emphasizes that civil and criminal law serve to maintain a harmonious society:

> In a literal sense, "my judgments" (*mishpatai*) means precisely civil and criminal law (*ha-dinin*)... Thus it says, "which a man performs and thereby lives." For these laws were given for the life of man, to foster his civil life and for the sake of peace. [CT: Lev. 18:4 - II, 99-100]

[7.23] Nahmanides returns to this point in distinguishing these laws, whose reasons are evident to all, from the statutes (*huqqim*) whose reasons are evident only through esoteric knowledge:

> Because the satutes (*huqqim*) are commandments whose reasons were not revealed to the masses, fools despise...them... but the ordinances (*mishpatim*) are something that everyone wants and needs, because the people have no civilization or society without the rule of law (*mishpat*). [CT: Lev. 26:15 - II, 187]

[7.24] The Seven Noahide Commandments belong to natural law; they are rationally self-evident:

> These matters [sexual immorality and robbery] and the rest of the Seven Commandments were commanded from the time of the first human being. The Rabbis derived them from hints in the verse (Gen. 2:16) "And the Lord God commanded humans [*ha-'adam*] saying [from every tree of the garden you may eat, but from the Tree of the Knowledge of Good and Evil you may not eat]." But God did not elaborate on these matters to them, for such elaborations were given to us at Sinai. On the face of it, these commandments are rational (*sikhliyot*). And every creature who recognizes his Creator should consider himself bound by (*lee-zaher*) them. [KR: *Torat ha-Shem Temimah* - I, 173]

The distinction of "rational commandments" (*sikhliyot*) from those known only from revelation (*shim'iyot*) is made by Saadiah Gaon (*ED*, 3.3; see J. Faur, *'Iyyunim be-Mishneh Torah le-ha-Rambam* [Jerusalem: Mosad Harav Kook, 1978], 115 ff.). But for Saadiah rational commandments pertain both to human relationships and to our relationship with God (*ED*, 3.1). Every area of human existence admits of rational understanding. There is no objective difference between what comes from reason and what comes from revelation (*ED*, Introduction, 6). The difference between reason and revelation is in *how* essentially the same truth is reached. With reason, the human knower is the active discoverer of truth; with revelation, the human knower is more passive, a recipient of truth. But for Nahmanides the rational commandments pertain only to human relations, and even there only partially. As regards our relationship with God, revelation does not just uncover what is already present but establishes the relationship. Like creation, it institutes a new reality rather than describing an old one. Thus Nahmanides draws the etymology of the word "covenant" (*berit*) from "creation" (*beriyyato shel 'olam*) [CT:intro. - I, 4 following Shir ha-Shirim Rabbah 1.29 re Deut. 4:13].

This historical emphasis is not ultimately consistent with the kabbalistic doctrine that the Torah is the revelation of the *primordial* being of God. For in the kabbalistic doctrine, all the commandments are participations in that divine life, so can be radically new and none pertains essentially to an interhuman reality. The inconsistency, to my knowledge, is one Nahmanides never overcame in his theology, as the author of the *Zohar* did, in effect, by eliminating the category of rational commandments altogether. Maimonides, on the other hand, also eliminated the distinction, from the opposite direction as it were, by seeing all the commandments as rational in essence. See D. Novak, *The Image of the Non-Jew in Judaism*, 278-80; I. Twersky, *Introduction to the Code of Maimonides* (New Haven: Yale University Press, 1980) 458-59.

[7.25] Nahmanides makes the same distinction in differentiating an ordinary Noahide from a resident-alien (*ger toshav*), one who observes as divine revelation the Seven Commandments as understood by the Jewish authorities. The ordinary Noahide observes them simply because they are rational (see Maimonides, *Hilkhot Melkahim*, 8.10-11; Novak, *The Image of the Non-Jew in Judaism*, 259-65).

> Let it be known that the Noahide mentioned throughout the Talmud *is* a resident-alien, except that a Noahide is one who simply behaves properly (*ke-hogan*) toward his fellow human beings according to these commandments, whereas a resident--alien actually came to a Jewish court and formally accepted them. This goes beyond the practice of other Noahides, who did not formally accept them. He is more punctilious (*medaqdeq*) about them... The other Noahides are in the category of those who observe even though they are not actually commanded to do so [B. 'Avodah Zarah 2b-3a]. But the resident-alien, who accepted them in a Jewish court, is one who observes these commandments as commandments. [*Hiddushei ha-Ramban ha-Shalem*: B. Makkot 9a, p. 61]

[7.26] Even natural law for Nahmanides is not simply natural. It is part of the God's plan for the created order:

> It is God's purpose to command justice be done among his creatures. For that is the reason he created them: that there should be justice and equity among them... If you panic and do violence, you have sinned against the Lord and violated his charge. [CT: Deut. 1:17 - II, 349]

[7.27] *Imitatio Dei*, moreover, requires imaginative application in concrete, specific circumstances, of the general principles of justice and equity laid down in the Torah:

> Even when God did not specifically command you, it should still be your intention to do what is good and right (*yashar*) in his eyes. For he loves the good and the right. This is a major principle. For it is impossible for the Torah to command all human actions and order every single interaction of one human being with another, to regulate every business transaction and improve every social and political matter. [CT: Deut. 6:18 - II, 376]

In CT: Lev. 19:2 (II, 115) Nahmanides expounded the need for an ordering of permitted sexual and ritual practices, pursuant to the larger end of holiness. Here he explains the ordering of permitted social and commercial practices, pursuant to the general end of justice. Natural law is seen as a participation in God's creative wisdom, which governs the universe.

[7.28] Even the observance of such "natural laws" involves divine providence:

> Indeed, all this is a high privilege of the judges of Israel and the assurance that God confirms their authority [*maskeem 'al yadam*] and is with them in matters of true judgment. [CT: Deut. 19:19 - II, 434]

The expression "confirms their authority" echoes the Talmudic dictum that God, after the fact, confirmed Moses' decision to break the first tablets of the Ten Commandments (Exod. 32:19). Moses had acted on his own assessment of the "needs of the hour," not on the basis of a divine decree, when he saw the people worshipping the Golden Calf (B. Shabbat 87a). There is much discussion in rabbinic sources about such personal judgments in times of crisis: Judicial integrity and discretion must be trusted in cases which the law cannot cover specifically (B. Sanhedrin 46a). But there is the ever present danger of abuses of power and a vigilante mentality jeopardizing the rule of law (B. Sanhedrin 82a; Maimonides, *Hilkhot Sanhedrin*, 24.4, 10). For Nahmanides, it seems, the best assurance that judges will use their discretion responsibly is for them to be keenly aware that their role is one of *imitatio Dei* (KR: *Torat ha-'Adam* - II, 41).

[7.29] The continuity between natural and supernatural goods is seen in the way the commandments serve both bodily and spiritual ends:

> Once again the Torah enlightens our eyes as to the mystery of generation... and so it is with all the ways of the Torah. For it commands all things good for the body according to the familiar order of the world, and all that are good for the soul in regard to its nature and in regard to the keeping of the commandments. For it is known that these foods are good for health and for healing. Other foods are harmful to the soul because of the traits they engender... Birds of prey are cruel, and their blood and flesh engender cruelty in the soul. Israel is commanded to be compassionate and loving to one another. So it was fitting (*ra'ui*) that this be prohibited to them... For all the ways of the Torah provide a benefit (*to'elet*) to body and soul. The Physician who knows how creatures are formed commanded this. [KR: *Torat ha-Shem Temimah* - I, 166-67]

The Physician, of course, is God.

[7.30] Thus not only political but even biological considerations are taken into account by the Torah's commandments.

> Scripture forbade sexual contact with a menstruant... in order to preserve the species... Physicians themselves say as much. [CT: Lev. 18:19 - II, 104]

[7.31] Nahmanides accepts Maimonides' biological rationale for the dietary prohibitions of the Torah, and even his historical rationale as well:

> The foods forbidden in the Torah are bad for the body too. Maimonides gave this reason in the *Moreh Nevukhim* [3.37]. It is like the reasons he gave for many other commandments, that these forbidden practices were used by magicians and sorcerers at that time for witchcraft. [CT: Lev. 19:23 - II, 125]

[7.32] Certain practices are prohibited because they are naturally loathsome. Glossing the rare pejorative use of *hesed* in the Torah's prohibition of incest, "If a man marries his sister... so that he sees her nakedness and she sees his nakedeness, it is a disgrace (*hesed*)" (Lev. 20:17), Nahmanides writes:

> According to the opinion of the commentators, *hesed* means 'shameful' (*herpah*); for men are naturally ashamed of this disgusting (*mekho'ar*) act. [CT: Lev. 20:17 - II, 131]

[7.33] Incest is rejected, even though certain types might seem to be permitted by the Noahide law. Thus, in commenting on the incest of Lot's daughters with their father, Nahmanides writes:

> They were shy (*tsenu'ot*) and did not want to tell their father to marry them, for a Noahide may marry his daughter. Alternatively, it was a disgusting thing (*mekho'ar*) in the eyes of those generations and it was not ever to be done. [CT: Gen. 19:32 - I, 119]

[7.34] Even Noahide law, fundamentally, comprises the elementary restraints that are the *sine qua non* of any society capable of sustaining human loyalty. Nevertheless, it is not specific enough to function as the content of any real legal system. In this respect Jewish civil and criminal law are similar to Noahide law:

> But he imposed on the Noahides the laws pertaining to theft, fraud, exploitation and the like... These are like the civil and criminal law (*ha-dinin*) given to Israel... Such commandments only restrain (*ha-meni'ah*) wrongdoing. [CT: Gen. 34:13 - I, 192]

[7.35] While a commandment may have a manifest natural aspect, it may simultaneously have an even more important mystical or supernatural aspect. That is always its ultimate ground:

> Know that sexual intercourse mentioned in the Torah is is something one should keep far away from; for it is disgusting, except for the preservation of the species... But the incestuous unions (*he-'arayot*) are statutes (*huqqim*), matters of the King's decree. This is something that enters the mind of the King, who in his wisdom and sovereignty knows the need and purpose of what he commanded but does not explain it to the people, except to the wisest of his counsellors. [CT: Lev.26:1 - II, 101]

[7.36] Even the norms that serve such obvious human requirements as maintaining good relations in society have deeper meanings. Thus restraint from harming one's neighbor can be understood as warranted by the natural need for social order. But the positive commandment to *love* one's neighbor does not follow from this. It requires special revelation:

> The reason for having a special commandment "love your neighbor as yourself" is that it is an unusual (*haflagah*) obligation. For the heart of a person will not accept that he has to love his neighbor like his own life. [CT: Lev. 19:17 - II, 119]

[7.37] Clearly Nahmanides believes that all God's commandments have reasons and are not simply expressions of arbitrary authority. They reflect the wisdom as well as the will of God. But only the civil and criminal laws are comprehensible by the canon of ordinary human experience. The other commandments have reasons that are more esoteric:

> The statutes are his decrees (*gezerotav*), and the ordinances are the civil and criminal laws (*dinin*). The former need more reinforcement because their reasons are hidden... But, in addition, the statutes and ordinances themselves are just and good for the civilization (*yishuv*) of the people and society. [CT: Deut. 4:3 - II, 361]

[7.38] Like Maimonides, Nahmanides vigorously opposes the view that any commandment is without specific reasons. If that were so, the commandments of God would be mere expressions of caprice. In truth all express God's wisdom in all its specificity. The difference between the two categories of commandments is just in how readily their reasons can be apprehended by unaided human reason:

> The intention is not that the decree of the King of kings should *ever* be without reason (*ta'am*)... but statutes (*huqqim*) are decrees of a King enacted in his kingdom, whose benefit (*to'elatam*) is not revealed to the people... Likewise the statutes of God: they are mysteries of his in the Torah which the people do not fully comprehend, as they do the ordinances (*mishpatim*). But all of them are reasonable, sound, and entirely purposeful. [CT: Lev. 19:19 - II, 120]

[7.39] Some transgressions are readily understood as offenses against human life and society. Others offend against deeper aspects of the divine life itself:

> For the Flood occurred on account of the corruption of the earth, and the Dispersion of Babel was because "they cut the plants," so they were punished by His great Name. [CT: Gen. 11:2 - I, 71]

'Cutting the plants' here refers to heresy arising from the adoption of private views of the divine life and its mysteries (B. Hagigah 14b). The metaphor, as Nahmanides understands it, guided by rabbinic opinion, is that the heretic cuts off growing plants from their proper roots when he forms opinions contrary to the Torah, the source of all truth (see, e.g., Ruth Rabbah 6.6).

[7.40] Nahmanides, as we have seen, devotes much attention to historical commandments. These symbolically commemorate the public miracles wrought by God, allowing later generations of Jews, who were not physically present when the original miracles occurred, to participate in those great experiences:

> These commandments are called "testimonies" (*'edot*), since they are a reminder of his wondrous acts and a testimony (*'edut*) of them. [CT: Deut. 6:20 - II, 376]

[7.41] Of the festivals, he writes:

> The essence (*'iqqar*) of these commandments is that these days be remembered and observed as a holiday from all exhausting labor. [CT: Num. 30:1 - II, 319]

[7.42] Great public miracles are rare because their impact would be diminished were they commonplace. But every generation of Jews must be linked to them:

> Because God will not perform a miracle or portent (*mofet*) in every generation before the eyes of every evidoer and nonbeliever, he commanded that we always preserve a memorial (*zikaron*) and a sign (*'ot*) of what our eyes saw. [CT: Exod. 13:16 - I, 346]

Again,

> The commandments called "testimonies" (*'edot*) are so named because they serve as a reminder (*zekher*) of God's wondrous deeds and are testimony (*'edut*) of them – like *matsah*, *sukkah*, Passover, the Sabbath, *tefillin*, and *mezuzah*... The intent is to inform our children, who ask [the meaning of what we are doing], that the Lord is the Creator, the Will and the Power, as was made clear to us in the Exodus from Egypt. This is the reason (*ta'am*) before our very eyes. For we are those who know and can testify from our experience of the signs and portents that the Lord our God is the God of heaven and earth; there is no one else... It is also good for us to perform the statutes (*ha-huqqim*). No statute entails anything bad, even though its reason has not been made explicit to everyone. [CT: Deut. 6:20 - II, 376-77]

The distinction between commemorative laws (*'edot*) and statutes (*huqqim*) is vivid here. The *'edot* have reasons evident to anyone familiar with the history of Israel. The *huqqim* have reasons that pertain to the inner life of God. That is why they are more mysterious.

[7.43] All of the commemorative commandments ultimately intend the act of creation, which no creature immediately experienced:

> He commanded us to make a sign (*siman*) and a perpetual memorial of this, to make known that God created all things. And this is the commandment of the Sabbath, which is a memorial of creation. [CT: Exod. 20:8 - I, 395]

[7.44] The indirect remembrance of creation and the direct remembrance of the Exodus are vitally related in the commemorative commandments:

> When we rest and refrain from work on the seventh day, we do not thereby directly have a remembrance (*zikaron*) of the Exodus from Egypt. Someone who merely sees us idle from work will not know this... It will, however, be a reminder (*zekher*) of creation that we rest on the day that the Lord rested and was refreshed. The truth is that the Exodus from Egypt teaches us of the eternal God (*Elohah qadmon*), who creates all that he desires, and who is capable of doing so... If doubt arises in your mind about the Sabbath's teaching as to God's creation, will and sovereignty, remember what your eyes saw in the Exodus from Egypt, which was itself a proof and a reminder for you. Indeed, the Sabbath is a reminder of the Exodus from Egypt; and the Exodus from Egypt is a reminder of the Sabbath. [CT: Deut. 5:15 - II, 367]

Nahmanides here implies that the commemorative commandments cannot be appreciated unless one is predisposed to appreciate the transcendence of God. The proper intent in keeping them increases faith, to be sure, but it also presupposes a basis in faith (CT: Gen. 14:10 - I, 85-85). Without such faith, one who keeps these commandments will be no more aware of their intent than a mere observer who sees Jews keeping the Sabbath and cannot infer from that fact alone that that what is seen is a memorial of the Exodus – let alone that it intends God's act of creation.

[7.45] Nahmanides explains that a convert who joins the people of Israel joins the historical memory of Israel through the performance of Israel's action-symbols:

> We know that the sojourners (*gerim*) who went forth from Egypt, the mixed multitude, perform the rite of the paschal lamb. For they too were included in the miracle. But those

> who converted afterwards, in the wilderness or in the Land of Israel, do fall under this obligation to perform the rite of the paschal lamb, since neither they nor their ancestors took part in the miracle... Thus it was necessary to obligate them to perform the rite of the paschal lamb in subsequent generations (*pesah dorot*), both in the wilderness and in the Land of Israel. [CT: Num. 9:14 - II, 227]

The commandments form an experiential link with the public miracles. So one need not have experienced the miracles directly, or even be descended from ancestors who did.

[7.46] The natural aspects of the Torah's commandments as *mishpatim* and their historical aspects as *'edot* can both be understood in terms of human need: the need to be part of the natural order biologically and of the social order politically. They also address the need to recognize the God who transcends nature in the governance of history:

> We hold... that there is a reason for all the commandments... to teach us good qualities of character... and to refine our souls... Accordingly, all of them are entirely for our benefit... This is a matter of consensus (*davar muskam*) in all the dicta of our Rabbis... the aim of all the commandments is to benefit us, not him, blessed and exalted be he. [CT: Deut. 22:6 - II, 448-49]

However, the two types of commandments mediate the relationship between God and Israel differently: the *mishpatim* through nature; the *'edot*, through history.

[7.47] Yet the view that the commandments fulfill human needs reaches only to the first level of meaning of the *mishpatim* and *'edot*. If all the commandments are ultimately participations in the divine life and if we ourselves are made in the image of God, then the commandments must reflect both a divine and a human reality. None simply serves human needs, but all together comprise our very being:

> There are only two things for us: "to fear God" (Eccl. 12:13) – in our hearts – "and to keep his commandments" – in our actions. Thus shall we be beloved by God "for this is the whole of man" (*ki zeh kol ha-'adam*). Awe is the root of the formation of a human being. His eyes and his head and all his limbs are nothing. The commandments are his body and his limbs and his soul. [KR: *Sermon on Kohelet* - I, 203]

If the commandments were seen simply as serving human nature, it would be assumed that *first* there is the reality, human nature, whose needs the commandments *then* serve. Human nature would transcend the commandments. This is how most of the rationalist theologians viewed the teleology of the commandments. But if the commandments themselves *constitute* human nature, if it does not even exist without them, then the ends of the commandments must transcend human nature. They can only be the inner needs of God.

[7.48] Some commandments are seen as introducing one directly into the inner life of the divine. These are the *huqqim*. They have a special immediacy and importance in that they respond to divine need. Nahmanides here expresses a doctrine (if he is not actually establishing it) which was much developed by later kabbalists, that God himself has a need to make his power and providence effective in creation and thus needs human cooperation (Meir ibn Gabbai, *'Avodat ha-Qodesh*, sec. 2). Commenting on the verse, "They shall know that I am the Lord their God, who brought them out of the land of Egypt to dwell (*le-shokhni*) in their midst" (Exod. 29:46), Nahmanides writes:

> There is in this matter a great mystery. For ostensibly the *Shekhinah* in Israel answers a human need (*tsorekh hedyot*) and not a divine need (*tsorekh Gavoah*). But, the fact is, as Scripture stated, "Israel, in you am I glorified" (Isaiah 49:3). [CT: Exod. 29:46 - I, 486-87]

In speaking of a "mystical meaning" (*sod*) here, Nahmanides alludes to the ultimate level of intelligibility of God's acts and the Torah's commandments, a level not accessible to ordinary students of the Torah, but only to those who have joined the heavenly company through prophecy or through authentic tradition (*kabbalah*).

[7.49] Thus Nahmanides argues that the commandments should be interpreted in terms of divine rather than human needs:

> Do not make yourself the root... "it is enough for the servant to be like the master" [B. Berakhot 58b]. As it is mine, so is it yours... According to deeper truth, it is like "they shall take for me (*li*) a heave offering" (Exod. 25:2). [CT: Lev. 25:23 - II, 179]

If the commandments essentially serve human needs, then man, not God, is the ultimate end and arbiter of revelation and creation. But when God implies that man must act in God's behalf, God's needs become paramount.

[7.50] In keeping with this theme, Nahmanides will assign reasons for the more mysterious commandments (*huqqim*), beyond the general rubrics that Maimonides set forth. In fact he places a much higher value on these commandments, since they involve intimate participation in God's life:

> In my opinion, there is a reason here like that of the sacrifices performed outside the Temple, like the goat sent out on Yom Kippur and by which the land is purged. That is why the sages counted the law of the ceremony of breaking the neck of a heifer (*'eglah 'arufah*) as one of the statutes. [CT: Deut. 21:4 - II, 440]

Expiation, which is the stated purpose of the ceremony, performed in a case of an unsolved murder (Deut. 21:8), is not just a matter of our becoming reconciled with God, but also a matter of inner divine reconciliation.

It is Maimonides, in the *Mishneh Torah*, who lists the law of the heifer with the broken neck as one of the *huqqim*, whose reason (*ta'am*) is not known (*Hilkhot Me'ilah*, 8.8), although one should not assume any of them serve no higher end (*sof 'inyanam*). In the rabbinic sources of the distinction between *mishpatim* and *huqqim*, this law is not included among the *huqqim* (*Sifra*: Aharei-Mot, ed. Weiss, 86a; B. Yoma 67b.). In the *Moreh Nevukhim* (3.40) Maimonides does supply a reason: The publicity involved in this unusual ceremony may elicit information about the perpetrator of the murder. For Maimonides all of the commandments have reasons, but all of the reasons address human needs. For Nahmanides some of the reasons involve divine needs. Maimonides, of course, would not admit that God has any needs at all.

[7.51] Often Nahmanides assigns two different reasons to a commandment, one involving a specific human need, the other indicating some divine need. The latter, derived from Kabbalah directly or by inference, is termed the *true* reason. This might seem to suggest that the other is false. But Nahmanides is open to a multiplicity of intentions within the Torah. He does not seek to impose a unitary interpretation (CT: Exod. 20:23 - I, 411; B. Sanhedrin 34a re Jer. 23:29; Bemidbar Rabbah 13.15 re Num. 7:79). What is not "true" as authentic kabbalistic teaching is still not false, but is often just less true, precisely because it is oriented toward humans rather than toward God.

The commemorative commandments, on the lower level, are understood as designed to remind humans whose ordinary frame of reference is the regularity of nature of the transcendent power of God. For that power was clearly made manifest in God's public miracles. But on a higher level the same commandments are understood as designed to enhance participation in the inner life of God by those saints whose normal frame of reference is this inner life itself, where they see their true location:

> In terms of truth (*'al derekh ha-'emet*), when this verse states, "because of what the Lord did for me (*li*, Exod. 13:8)," it has the same sense as, "this is my God (*Eli*) whom I glorify" (Exod. 15:2). For the sake of his Name and his honor he did these things for us and brought us out of Egypt. Thus it shall be for you a sign on your strong, outstretched arm. Its reason (*ke-ta'am*) is expressed in the verse "for you are the splendor (*tif'eret*) of his strength" (Psalms 89:18)... Its purpose is to indicate complete unification [*she-ha-kol ba-kol*] – that is, the presence of the four passages from the Torah that pertain to God and Israel are placed in one compartment in the *tefillin* worn on the arm... Now I shall tell you a reason (*ta'am*) for many commandments... Many people deny the very root of faith (*kofrim be-'iqqar*) and say that the world is eternal... So when God chooses a community or an individual, he demonstrates (*mofet*) his supernatural power to them by changing the familiar order of the nature of the world, so that all of these erroneous opinions may be nullified... But because God does not perform a sign (*'ot*) or demonstration in every generation... he commanded us to make a continual reminder (*tamid zikaron*) of what our eyes saw. [CT: Exod. 3:16 - I, 345-46]

Elsewhere (CT: Deut. 13:2 - II, 404), Nahmanides distinguishes a "sign" (*'ot*) from a "demonstration" (*mofet*). The former is a predicted event; the latter, a radically new miraculous event (*davar mehudash*), performed through a prophet without prediction (cf. Rashi *ad loc.*). The historical condition of faith is needed by ordinary people, who are usually separated from God – unlike saints who need no such condition. Nahmanides remarks "that faith is now memory" (*ha-zekhirah 'attah – Notes on Maimonides' Sefer ha-Mitsvot*, neg. no. 1, p. 261). That is, for most people, to believe is to remember actively. So symbolic reenactment of the public miracles through the commemorative commandments is the very heart of faith.

[7.52] Nahmanides is an important source for the kabbalistic doctrine of a substantial connection uniting – not just relating – God and Israel. Concerning the verse, "And he called him God (*'El*) God of Israel" (Gen. 33:20), he writes:

> The truth here is according to the rabbinic interpretation [B. Megillah 18a]: "How do we know that God called Jacob God (*El*)? – For it is written here, "He called him 'God'." There is a great secret (*sod gadol*) in this, as the Rabbis said elsewhere [Bereshit Rabbah 79.8], "He [Jacob] said to him [God], "you are God among the heavenly beings and I am God among the earthly beings." Here we have a hint of what the

> sages constantly said, that the image (*eikonin*) of Jacob is engraved upon the divine throne [Bereshit Rabbah 78.3]. [CT: Gen. 33:20 - I, 189]

The same Midrash is critical of Jacob's calling himself God among earthly beings. It takes the rape of his daughter Dinah, mentioned immediately thereafter, as a punishment of this arrogance. But Nahmanides reads the passage as implying that God himself called Jacob divine. Relying on the apparent ambiguity of the pronoun reference, he follows an interpretation found in the Babylonian Talmud, which treats God, not Jacob, as calling Jacob God [B. Megillah 18a]. The *Zohar* (Toldot, 1:138a), undoubtedly, following Nahmanides, attempts to make the Midrash follow the Talmud more smoothly by reworking the midrashic text to have it say that God designated himself as divine above and Jacob as divine below (cf. B. Berakhot 10a). All this lays a foundation for the radical kabbalistic interpretation of everything in the Torah that seems to serve human needs as in truth serving divine needs.

[7.53] This idea became a cornerstone of kabbalistic theology. It implies that Israel is an indispensible participant in the divine life. Nahmanides brings out this entailment in discussing the Talmudic view that that Moses' prophetic vision was far clearer and more direct than that of any other prophet. Thus Moses could see the connection between Israel and God more clearly than any other human being:

> In my humble opinion, when Scripture says, " [For You O Lord are in the midst of this people] visible to the eye are You O Lord..." (Num. 14:14), the term 'eye' (*'ayin*) refers to a vision (*mar'eh*), that which is seen. Thus the interpretation of this verse is that Moses our master, peace be upon him, said to God, "Is not your great Name in the midst of this people? For the vision within the vision is your great Name, may it be exalted and blessed. Indeed, you are attached to the assembly of Israel (*knesset yisrael*), so it is impossible to expunge them, as Scripture says: "for my Name is within them (*be-qirbo*)" (Exod. 23:21). [*Hiddushei ha-Ramban*: B. Yevamot 49b, p. 236]

The vision of Israel, in its true character, is a vision of God, even if never adequate to God's full reality. "Seeing" God *within* Israel, then, is seeing Israel as indispensible to the divine life. God's being in the midst of Israel means that Israel cannot be conceived without its intimate connection to God. But God (as far as he can be conceived) cannot be conceived apart from Israel. In his *Commentary on the Torah* on this verse, Nahmanides returns to this interpretation and calls it the true, kabbalistic doctrine (CT: Num. 14:4 - II, 248). In another comment he emphasizes that God's presence in Israel is connected to that which is above (*mehubar le-ma'alah*), i.e., to the highest levels of the divine life (CT: Exod. 23:21 - I, 443).

[7.54] Nahmanides' distinction between the inner and outer meanings of the commandments acquires richer significance in his explanation of the essential difference between an oath (*shevu'ah*) and a vow (*neder*):

> In a vow one swears by the life of the King; in an oath one swears by the King himself" (CT: Num. 30:3 - II, 323).

The distinction has a rabbinic source (Sifre: Bemidbar, no. 153). Nahmanides uses it in his theology to signify our relationship with God himself, over and above our relationship with God as Creator of effects in the world, what might be called God's "outer life." As Scripture and the Rabbis taught, the Torah was accepted by the people of Israel, at Sinai and on the plains of Moab, through an oath. For Nahmanides, this means that observance of the commandments brings the Jewish people into the inner being of God. Thus, the Torah is more than the will of God:

> And there also God said to Israel, "When I *sold* you my Torah, as it were, I was sold with it." [CT: Exod. 25:3 - I, 454]

The rabbinic source for this comment is Shemot Rabbah 33.1. For an analysis of the theme in rabbinic theology, see D. Novak, *Halakhah in a Theological Dimension*, 121 ff.

[7.56] Along these lines, Nahmanides made a point, considerably developed by the later kabbalists, that the Torah is made up of God's own names (see CT: Intro. - I, 6). In other words, in the Torah God is ultimately speaking of himself and his own needs. The Torah is directed not merely to the human situation of its recipients. In truth it is their opportunity to participate in the divine life. Every seemingly mundane aspect of its observance is symbolic of God's higher reality, which encompasses all things. The view that Nahmanides consistently discovers in hints of this kind is one that we would call panentheistic: the world is contained within God, but God also transcends it (Bereshit Rabbah 68.9 re Gen. 28:11):

> The Rabbis call the language of the Torah "the language of the holy" (*lashon ha-qodesh*). For the words of the Torah and the prophecies and all the words of holiness, all of them were spoken in that language... in it his holy names are called out... and through it he created his world. [CT: Exod. 30:13 - I, 502]

[7.57] The Sanctuary (*mishkan*) is the visual symbol of the world created through the divine names. Its construction parallels that of creation itself:

> The mystery of the Sanctuary is that... Bezalel knew how to combine the letters whereby heaven and earth were created. [CT: Exod. 31:2 - I, 502]

[7.58] Moreover, the Sanctuary and the Sabbath are opposite sides of the same coin, the Sanctuary indicating the positive side of divine creativity, and the Sabbath its negative side, since most of the laws of the Sabbath are prohibitions. The two institutions are paradigmatic of all the commandments. Commenting on the juxtaposition of the Sanctuary and the Sabbath in Lev. 26:1-2, Nahmanides writes:

> The Rabbis hinted that all the commandments are included in the Sabbath and the Sanctuary. [CT: Lev. 26:1 - II, 182]

The essential connection between the two is made when the Rabbis identify the 39 categories of labor forbidden on the Sabbath with the 39 categories of labor required in the building of the Sanctuary (B. Shabbat 97a; Mekhilta: Va-yak'hel, ad init. 345, re Exod. 35:1).

[7.59] Nahmanides argues against Maimonides' treatment of the *Shekhinah* as a created entity (*Moreh*, 1.27). He takes this presence to be part of the Godhead. And because the Sanctuary is called the abode of the *Shekhinah* he regards the whole ritual of the Temple as a participation in the divine life. This point became a *leitmotif* in Kabbalah.

> Maimonides said that Onqelos [the Aramaic translator of the Torah noted for his avoidance of anthropomorphisms] asserted that the movement [ascribed in the Torah to God] and the manifestation of divine glory (*kavod*) – all refer to something created (*nivra*)... God forbid that anything called *Shekhinah* or divine glory should be a created entity, external to God himself, blessed be he, as Maimonides supposed in regard to this passage and many others in his book [*Moreh Nevukhim*]. For Onqelos translated the Scriptural passage, "if Your face (*panekha*) does not go [with us] (Exod. 33:15) as "if Your *Shekhinah* does not go with us." Moses did not want any created glory to go with him, but only the glorious God himself. For God had already said to him, "Behold, my angel will walk before you" (Exod. 33:14). But Moses did not want this; he wanted God himself in his own glory to walk with him (Exod. 33:15). [CT: Gen. 46:1 - I, 250]

Chapter 8

Eschatology

[8.1] For Nahmanides, the ultimate goal of the Torah and commandments is to bring the world back to its primordial condition, under the direct governance of God. The process of attaining this goal began with the redemption of Israel from Egypt and will culminate in the world to come:

> In the past I and my court of justice (*u-vet dini*) went before them... but in the future age (*le-'atid la-vo*) it will be Myself alone... The mystical meaning (*sod*) of this midrash [Shemot Rabbah 19.7] is, as I have stated, that in the first redemption God was with them by day; his court of justice, by night. But in the future age, his court of justice will be subsumed in his mercy... which is God's unique Name.... everything will be united in God's unique attribute of mercy (*middat rahamim*). [CT: Exod. 14:21 - I, 348]

The Rabbis often glossed the name *Elohim* as designating God's attribute of justice; and the tetragrammaton (YHWH), God's attribute of mercy (see A. Marmorstein, *The Old Rabbinic Doctrine of God* [New York: Ktav, 1968], 43 ff.). The theme that strict justice will be overcome by mercy is also frequently stressed (e.g., B. Berakhot 7a), but usually in a human context. The Rabbis typically apply the attributes of justice and mercy to the task of explaining God's relationship to his creatures. For the kabbalists, however, they become inner states of God's being, hypostatized attributes, with their own dynamic interrelations, *into* which human events are incorporated (see Scholem, *On the Kabbalah and its Symbolism*, 94). Thus the final redemption is primarily a reordering of God's inner nature, the fulfillment of God's own history. Only subsequently is it a reordering of human realities.

[8.2] The phrase 'world to come,' for Nahmanides, signifies a future age, not yet experienced in the past, although portended by its saving events. Its reality is temporal, unlike the world to come of Maimonides, which is an eternal, transcendent realm, a "world-beyond," existing timelessly alongside this world (*ha-'olam ha-zeh* - *Hilkhot Teshuvah*, 8.8). For Maimonides, the righteous person comes to the world-beyond. But for Nahmanides, the future world comes to replace this world. The temporality of cosmic fulfillment for Nahmanides expresses his great emphasis on history:

> Behold, the Garden of Eden and the world to come are signified here to those who understand these things. These places are where all blessings are consummated. This consummation will not occur until all Israel do the will of their Father and the building of heaven and earth is completed by God and us. Know that Israel has never fully attained these blessings, collectively or individually. No one's merit has risen to this level... That is why you will find that the Rabbis see in these verses an allusion to the future age... This has not yet been achieved, but it will be, in the time of completion (*ba-zman ha-shlemut*). [CT: Lev. 26:12 - II, 186]

[8.3] Although the world-to-come is everlasting (*qayyam*), it is created, not eternal (KR: *Torat ha-'Adam*: Sha'ar ha-Gemul - II, 303), a historical succession rather than a realm ever present.

[8.4] The world to come is the culmination and fulfillment of history:

> It has been made clear that the world to come is not a world of disembodied souls (*'olam ha-neshamot*) but a world which is created and then endures. Those who are resurrected there will exist in body and soul... The subsistence of those who merit the splendor of God will be like that of the soul in the body in this world... But this soul will be like that of the angels in its union (*be-hityahdah*) with higher knowledge... The subrdination of body to soul will nullify the body's powers... so that the body will subsist like the soul, no longer eating or drinking, just as Moses subsisted for forty days on Mount Sinai. [KR: *Torat ha-'Adam*: Sha'ar ha-Gemul - II, 303-04]

[8.5] For Maimonides, resurrection of the dead is a dogma in which a Jew must believe, even though there is no rational evidence for it. It is a possibility open to God's creative transcendence of nature, but it need never actually occur (see *Ma'amar Tehiyyat ha-Metim*, ch. 8; *Moreh Nevukhim*, 2.25). Nor is it the ultimate aim of all human strivings. That end is the disembodied world to come, whose existence Maimonides holds to be rationally evident (*Hilkhot Teshuvah*, ch. 8). He is quite critical of those who think that the ultimate beatitude hinted in Scripture and discussed by the Rabbis is bodily resurrection rather than spiritual immortality in the world to come (*Ma'amar Tehiyyat ha-Metim*, ch. 2). But for Nahmanides, there is no difference between the two realms:

> Any commandment in the Torah, whose reward is mentioned along with it entails the resurrection of the dead [Hullin 142a]... That means that bodies do not return to dust forever... [one might think that once dead] the body no longer has any function (*po'el raiq*), but God does nothing in vain (*po'el battel*). The answer to all of this is that the purpose the body was created for was its function at the time of the resurrection, as mentioned above. For God does not want it to be destroyed after physical death. Furthermore, the bodily form has many mysteries about it, for its formation was not pointless (*hefqer*) or without reason. [KR: *Torat ha-'Adam*: Sha'ar ha-Gemul - II, 305]

[8.6] If the body loses its physical functions in the future realm, what is the point of its being resurrected at all? How does this differ from the Platonic idea of the immortality of the soul, that sees the soul's fulfillment in its being finally rid of the body altogether (*Phaedo* 66C)? Nahmanides replies that the body, however much spiritualized, still sustains the soul's temporality and thus its individuality. Without the body, the soul would simply merge into a panpsychic unity with all other righteous souls. How, then, could any soul be rewarded in the world to come for its own righteousness? This view of Nahmanides on the resurrection of the dead is clearly a compromise between the physicality of many of the Rabbis (B. Sanhedrin 90b *et seq.*; *Tanhuma*: Vayigash, no. 9, ed. S. Buber, 104b-105a) and the more spiritual views of others (B. Berakhot 17a). The standing of the more spiritualized rabbinic views was considerably enhanced when theologians like Nahmanides, who were usually suspicious of Greek metaphysics, accorded partial acceptance to the body-soul dualism that arose ultimately from the thinking of Plato. But despite his partial acceptance of dualism, Nahmanides differs pointedly with Ibn Gabirol, Maimonides and other Jewish rationalists, who professed spiritual immortality at the expense of physical resurrection. Nahmanides regards that approach as an unwarranted departure from tradition. He praises Saadiah for closely adhering to rabbinic tradition on this point (KR: *Torat ha-'Adam*: Sha'ar ha-Gemul - II, 311) and insists that the physical resurrection be taken absolutely seriously:

> The eternal survival of the body is not the doctrine of the philosophers, nor of certain Sages of the Torah... they believe, by virtue of their speculation (*be-'iyunam*), in the eternal survival of the species. But we can believe, by virtue of our tradition, in

> the eternal survival of the individual (*ha-perat*), by God's exalted will. [KR: *Torat ha-'Adam*: Sha'ar ha-Gemul - I, 306]

[8.7] The soul's need for the body is never transcended. To assert any such transcendence would cast aspersions on the value of creation:

> One might object to us that the body is composed of organs that exist to sustain the activity of the soul. These are classified into three divisions: ...organs of nourishment, of procreation, and of general sustenance... But once this purpose (*takhlit*) is no longer extant, in the world-to-come... the body no longer serves any need and should no longer exist, since God's work is not for naught. Our response is that this creation is for the time of the resuurection, when the organs will be needed for these functions once again. For God does not intend that they should be ruined hereafter... the survival of the body and the survival of the soul is through their becoming united with supernal knowledge (*be-da'at 'elyon*). [KR: *Torat ha-'Adam*: Sha'ar ha-Gemul - II, 305]

[8.8] With an extensive marshalling of rabbinic sources, Nahmanides presents the eschatological order:

> The reward of souls and their survival in the world of souls (*ba-'olam ha-nefashot*) is called the Garden of Eden by our Rabbis. Sometimes they call it "ascent" (*'aliyah*), or "the academy above" (*yeshivah shel ma'alah*). Then come the days of the Messiah, which are still within the realm of this world. At their end is the final judgment and the resurrection of the dead, which is the requital, involving both body and soul. It is the fundamental principle (*ha-'iqqar ha-gadol*) for all those who hope in God, the world to come, to which the body as well as the soul will return. The soul cleaves close (*be-hadbaqah*) to divine knowledge in the Garden of Eden, the world of souls. It then ascends with great insight into God from within itself. And the survival of the soul and body together is everlasting. [KR: *Torat ha-'Adam*: Sha'ar ha-Gemul - II, 306]

[8.9] Much closer to rabbinic tradition than Maimonides, Nahmanides conceives the world to come as essentially temporal, succeeding this world. The resurrection of the dead marks the final transition from this world to the world to come:

> Concerning the world to come, which is the final reward for observance of the *mitsvot*, it is in doubt... whether it is the world of souls, and reward reaches each of them immediately after death... or whether it is the world wherein reward will be created for body and soul, or for the soul alone at this new time... But we are taught that the world to come is the world of reward for those whom God resurrects. It is not, however, the world of souls called the Garden of Eden. Rather, it is the world of the resurrection. [KR: *Torat ha-'Adam*: Sha'ar ha--Gemul - II, 302]

Maimonides' transhistorical view of the world to come, which Nahmanides so forcefully rejects, was criticized during Maimonides' lifetime by his best known contemporary critic Abraham ben David of Posquières (Rabad). Citing B. Sanhedrin 97a, which interprets Isaiah 2:17 – "the Lord will be exalted on that day (*ba-yom ha-hu*)" – Rabad (note on *Hilkhot Teshuvah*, 8.8) speaks of the world to come as "a new world" (*'olam hadash*) in an objective, temporal sense. Nahmanides similarly states that the world to come is a world which "God will create in the future (*le-hadsho*), after (*le-'ahar*) the days of the Messiah and the resurrection of the dead" (KR: *Torat ha-'Adam*: Sha'ar ha-Gemul - II, 302). For Maimonides, the newness of the world to come is subjective, representing the experience of human beings who newly apprehend what is in itself eternal. This fundamental difference is glossed over by Joseph Karo in his note in *Kesef Mishneh*, *ad loc.*, where he responds to Rabad's critique. But Rabad's comment reveals Nahmanides' greater faithfulness to the rabbinic sources. As one text (cited by neither Rabad nor Nahmanides) clearly puts it, "This world departs and the world to come enters" (Y. Yevamot 15.2/14d re Ps. 140:8). For the radical character of Maimonides' view of history, see D. Novak, "Does Maimonides have a Philosphy of History?" in ed. Samuelson, *Studies in Jewish Philosophy*, 397 ff.)

[8.10] By emphasizing the timelessness of the world to come, Maimonides deemphasizes God's direct meting out of reward and punishment in history. For him the ultimate punishment is separation from the eternal realm of bliss, resultant from separating oneself from it during this life. Nahmanides criticizes Maimonides' seeming departure from rabbinic eschatology for a view closer to that of Plato (*Phaedo* 67C):

> In another place (*Commentary on the Mishnah*: Sanhedrin, ch. 10 [*Heleq*], introduction) Maimonides avows ideas that are confusing... namely, that the great punishment means that the soul is cut off and lost and does not survive, and that is what the Torah means by *karet* (excision)... since whoever is drawn after bodily pleasures and casts the truth behind him, letting falsehood triumph over truth, shall lose that exalted state (*ha-*

> *-ma'aleh ha-hu*), leaving but his mortal body alone... But these ideas are not satisfactory (*nohim*) in our opinion. [KR: *Torat ha-'Adam*: Sha'ar ha-Gemul - II, 292]

The reason Maimonides' thoughts are not satisfactory is that the Rabbis speak of a place always existent (*matsui tamid*) for punishment, *and* of a future time when the nations will be judged.

[8.11] Both the Garden of Eden and the world to come are beyond ordinary nature. But the Garden of Eden is a physical site where souls are rewarded. The world to come is that state of being, after the resurrection, when spiritualized bodies enjoy everlasting bliss. The Garden of Eden, then, is the anteroom of the world to come:

> It is said that the reward of all the commandments and the good requital (*ha-gemul ha-tov*) is rooted in the world to come, as is evident from the words of our Rabbis. But the first reward that reaches a person after death is the Garden of Eden. This parallels what we explained concerning Hell (*Gehinnom*), which is the punishment that reaches a wicked person immediately (*miyyad*) upon death. This is what you find throughout the writings of the Rabbis – that the Garden of Eden is the counterpart of Hell. [KR: *Torat ha-'Adam*: Sha'ar ha-Gemul - II, 294]
>
> It is a principle established in the Torah and expounded by the Sages that the Garden of Eden exists in this world in a particular geographic spot... Geographers (*anshei middot*) say that it lies exactly on the equator. [Sha'ar ha-Gemul - II, 295]

Nahmanides is adamant that on this question rabbinic *aggadot* must be taken literally (Sha'ar ha-Gemul - II, 296, 298, 304), although elsewhere (KR: *Disputation*, secs. 22-39 - I, 306-08) he argues that many *aggadot* should be taken figuratively, and in some cases simply rejected. His clear criterion here is that an essential doctrine seems to him to be at stake. What really exists requires a description adequate to it. (For Nahmanides' view of *aggadot* in general as vehicles of normative kabbalistic doctrine, see E. R. Wolfson, "By Way of Truth.")

[8.12] Predictably, Nahmanides locates the Garden of Eden in the Land of Israel, whose sanctity reflects its linking this world to the world to come:

> The first human being, the immediate work of the hands of God, who was the choicest of the human species in understanding and knowledge, was made to dwell by God, blessed be he, in the choicest place for the pleasure and wellbeing of the

body. He depicted in this portentous place all the work of the upper world. The Garden of Eden is the world of souls in material form. Thus, from it one might understand the constitution of every creature: bodily, spiritual (*nafshi*), and angelic... Also, the Garden of Eden is the most significant place in the lower world (*ha-'olam ha-shafal*), for it is the center of the world, leading directly to the upper world. So those who are there will see divine visions more frequently than from any other place on earth. For the fact is, as we believe, that the Land of Israel and Jerusalem are the most auspicious places, especially suited for prophecy because of this direct linkage – all the more so with the Temple, which is the throne of the Lord. [KR: *Torat ha-'Adam*: Sha'ar ha-Gemul - II, 296]

[8.13] Nahmanides anticipates the objection that a physical Eden would have no real connection with the non-physical world to come:

> You may say, 'It is obvious from all the rabbinic sources that the Garden of Eden is in this lower world, so what then is the reward of souls there? For what is beneficial to souls is not physical and is not to be had anywhere in the lower world.' But we have already explained that this term has a double meaning (*kaful*): It is a garden (*gan*) and a delight (*'eden*). That is how it got its name. It is the place where these lower beings can receive from the upper world... Its mystery is deep, open only to those who have received the teaching of faith (*meqabblei ha-'emunah*). But our sages explain it as the place of souls (B. Shabbat 152b), where the souls of the righteous are stored beneath God's throne of glory. [KR: *Torat ha-'Adam*: Sha'ar ha-Gemul - II, 297]

[8.14] Thus the delights of the Garden of Eden are spiritual, even though the place itself is physical:

> During the twelve months [that the soul remains under physical influence – see B. Kiddushin 31b and Rashi *ad loc.*] the portion of the soul that is in the Garden of Eden derives its delight from the world above it, although it still inclines toward physicality (*notah le-gashmiyut*). It was not the sense of our Rabbis that souls enjoy the fruits of that Garden or bathe in its rivers. Rather their intent was that it is the Gateway to Heaven (*sha'ar ha-shamayim*), where one is "to bask in light everlasting" (Job 33:30). Thus it is said of one who stands in Jerusalem that his soul is clothed with the holy spirit, that prophetic agency (*mal'akhut nevu'ah*), by God's will, whether through dreams or

> visions, is more accessible there than to one who stands in an impure land [B. Shabbat 14a]. The apprehension available to the soul from that place raises itself up to connection (*devequt*) with the upper world and apprehension of spiritual delight. [KR: *Torat ha-'Adam*: Sha'ar ha-Gemul - II, 298]

[8.15] Nahmanides asserts that the world to come will arrive only when there is sufficient merit (*zekhut*) in Israel:

> Know that a man's life in the commandments is proportioned to his proclivity to them. For one who performs the commandments not for their own sake but in order to receive a reward will live in this world "many days" because of them... But those who engage in the commandments out of love and do what is right and proper in matters of this world... will merit a good life in this world according to the normal way (*ke-minhag*) of the world and in the world to come, where their merit will be complete... The children of the world to come will arise at the time of the resurrection. [CT: Lev. 18:4 - II, 100]

[8.16] The world to come will restore the world to its pristine condition, as it was before it was corrupted by sin:

> Thus Scripture says of the days of the redeemer of the stock of Jesse that peace will return to the world, carnage (*ha-teref*) will cease... and the world will revert its primordial nature. [CT: Lev. 26:6 - II, 183]

[8.17] Sin removes humanity from its original condition of grace:

> For the soul that sins is cut off because of its sin, but other souls remain in God's presence in heavenly splendor. [CT: Lev. 18:29 - II, 114]

[8.18] The reason for commandments about the dead is that humans were created to live forever. Only because of sin did death intervene between creation and resurrection in the world to come. So mourning is in reality for the presence of sin and its deadly effects in the world:

> For man's orginal destiny (*toldat ha-'adam*) was to live forever, but through the primal sin (*he-het ha-qadmoni*) all became mortal... That is why it is right for us to understand mourning as an act of worship of our God. [KR: *Torat ha-'Adam*: intro. - II, 12]

[8.19] By introducing death, sin disrupted the divine creative process:

> For it is God's work to be active in the business of the world, in the perpetuation of species. That is God's desire in creating us to endure forever. [KR: *Torat ha-'Adam*: intro. - II, 14]

[8.20] Considering original sin, Nahmanides distinguishes between physically inherited mortality and an actual moral taint. Despite our inherited mortality, sin itself is an individual responsibility. The point bears a special gravemen in the context of Nahmanides' polemic against Christianity:

> It would be outrageous (*halilah*) for God if the righteous were to be punished in Hell because of the sin of the first man, their father – that my soul should be akin to the soul of Pharaoh, as it is to the soul of my own father! My soul will not enter Hell because of Pharaoh's sin! But bodily chastisements arise because my body stems from my father and mother. And when it was decreed that they [Adam and Eve] should be mortal (*benei mavet*), their descendents thenceforth were made mortal by nature. [KR: *Disputation*, sec. 45 - I, 310]

The point elaborated later, in CT: Gen. 2:17 (I, 37-38), that God's sanction on the first pair for eating from the Tree of the Knowledge of Good and Evil was to change an immortal to a mortal nature (Gen. 3:19). The Rabbis similarly taught that not everyone dies because of some individual sin. For a few exceptional individuals, death comes only through inheritance of the mortality resultant from Adam's sin (B. Baba Batra 17a; *Midrash ha-Gadol*: Bereshit on Gen. 3:23, ed. Margaliot [Jerusalem: Mosad Ha-Rav Kook, 1947], 110).

[8.21] Jewish eschatology expects redemption both in this world and in the world to come. But the former is subordinate to the latter:

> Our ultimate requital (*takhlit gemulenu*) is not the Messianic Age and eating the fruits of the Land... Nor is it the sacrifices and the service of the Temple... Rather, our sights (*mabitenu*) are on the world to come and the soul's delight in the Garden of Eden and escape from the torment of Hell. Even so, we hold firm to redemption in this world; for it is upheld as true among those who were masters of the Torah and prophecy... For we await it in hope of reaching nearness to God by being in his Sanctuary with his priests and prophets, augmenting whatever purity and holiness may be in us, by being in the chosen land in the company of the *Shekhinah*. This is more

> than we can attain today, exiled among peoples who cause us to sin.... For in the days of the Messiah the evil inclination will be destroyed, so that we may reach the truth as it is... This is the essence of our desire and yearning for the days of the Messiah. [KR: *Sefer ha-Ge'ulah* - I, 279-80]

[8.22] Because Nahmanides awaits God's miraculous action in this world, he does not defer all reward and punishment to a transcendent realm:

> There are sins for which God's judgment and righteous decrees exact punishment in this world, and sins for which punishment is exacted in the world to come. Similarly, there are meritorious deeds for which the Lord of requitals (*ba'al ha-gemul*) gives recompense in the world to come. [KR: *Torat ha-'Adam*: Sha'ar ha-Gemul - II, 264]

Nahmanides here chooses between two rabbinic opinions regarding reward in this world, one stating that all reward is otherwordly (M. Kiddushin 1.10; B. Kiddushin 39b; Y. Kiddushin 1.7/61b re Job 37:23; Hullin 142a re Exod. 20:12 and Deut. 22:7); and the other stating that some or most reward is this-worldly (B. Kiddushin 39b and Tos., s.v. *matnitin*; M. 'Avot 4.1 re Ps. 128:2; *Midrash Aggadah*: Ve-'ethanan, ed. S. Buber, 125). Clearly, Nahmanides prefers the second view.

Selected Bibliography

Martin Buber, *I and Thou*, tr. Walter Kaufmann, New York: Scribner's, 1970

—— *Two Types of Faith*, tr. N. P. Goldhawk, New York: Collier, 1961.

Louis Ginzberg, *Legends of the Jews*, Philadelphia: JPS, 1925.

L. E. Goodman, ed., *Neoplatonism and Jewish Thought,* Albany: SUNY Press, 1992.

Judah Halevi, *Kuzari*, tr. H. Hirschfeld, New York: Schocken, 1964.

David Weiss Halivni, *Meqorot u-Mesorot*, Tel Aviv: Dvir, 1968.

Abraham Joshua Heschel, *God in Search of Man*, New York: Farrar, Straus and Cudahy, 1955.

—— *Man Is Not Alone*, Philadelphia: JPS, 1951.

M. Idel, *Kabbalah: New Perspectives*, New Haven: Yale University Press, 1988.

David Novak, *Halakhah in a Theological Dimension*, Chico: Scholars Press, 1985.

—— *Jewish-Christian Dialogue: A Jewish Justification*, New York: Oxford University Press, 1989.

—— *Law and Theology in Judaism*, New York: KTAV, 1974.

Saadiah Gaon, *The Book of Beliefs and Opinions*, tr. S. Rosenblatt, New Haven: Yale University Press, 1948.

—— *The Book of Theodicy: Translation and Commentary on the Book of Job*, tr. with commentary, L. E. Goodman, New Haven: Yale University Press, 1988.

Norbert Samuelson, ed., *Studies in Jewish Philosophy: Collected Essays of the Academy for Jewish Philosophy 1980-1985*, Lanham, MD: University Press of America, 1989.

Gershom Scholem, *Ha-Kabbalah be-Gerona*, Jerusalem: Hebrew University Student Federation, 1964.

—— *Major Trends in Jewish Mysticism*, 3rd rev. ed., New York: Schocken, 1961.

—— *On the Kabbalah and Its Symbolism*, tr. R. Manheim, New York: Schocken, 1969.

—— *Origins of the Kabbalah*, ed. R. J. Z. Werblowsky; tr. A. Arkush, Philadelphia: JPS, 1987.

I. Tishby, *Mishnat ha-Zohar* 2nd ed., Jerusalem: Mosad Bialik, 1961.

Isadore Twersky, ed., *Rabbi Moses Nahmanides (Ramban): Explorations in his Religious and Literary Virtuosity*, Cambridge: Harvard University Press, 1983

E. R. Wolfson, "By Way of Truth: Aspects of Nahmanides' Kabbalistic Hermeneutic," *AJS Review* 14, 1989.

List of Abbreviations

AJS — Association for Jewish Studies

B. — Talmud Bavli

CT — Nahmanides, *Commentary on the Torah*, ed. C. B. Chavel (Jerusalem: Mosad Harav Kook, 1959-63).

ED — Saadiah, *Sefer ha-Nivhar ba-'Emunot ve-De'ot*

JLA — *Jewish Law Annual*

JPS — Jewish Publication Society

JTS — Jewish Theological Society of America

KR — Nahmanides, *Kitvei Ramban*, ed. Chavel (Jerusalem: Mosad Harav Kook, 1963).

M. — Mishnah

T. — Talmud

Y. — Talmud Yerushalmi

Index of Names and Subjects

Index of Passages

Biblical

www.ingramcontent.com/pod-product-compliance
Lightning Source LLC
Chambersburg PA
CBHW021109090426
42738CB00006B/572

* 9 7 8 1 9 3 0 6 7 5 5 9 9 *